M000214309

BEADAZZLED

Where Beads & Inspiration Meet

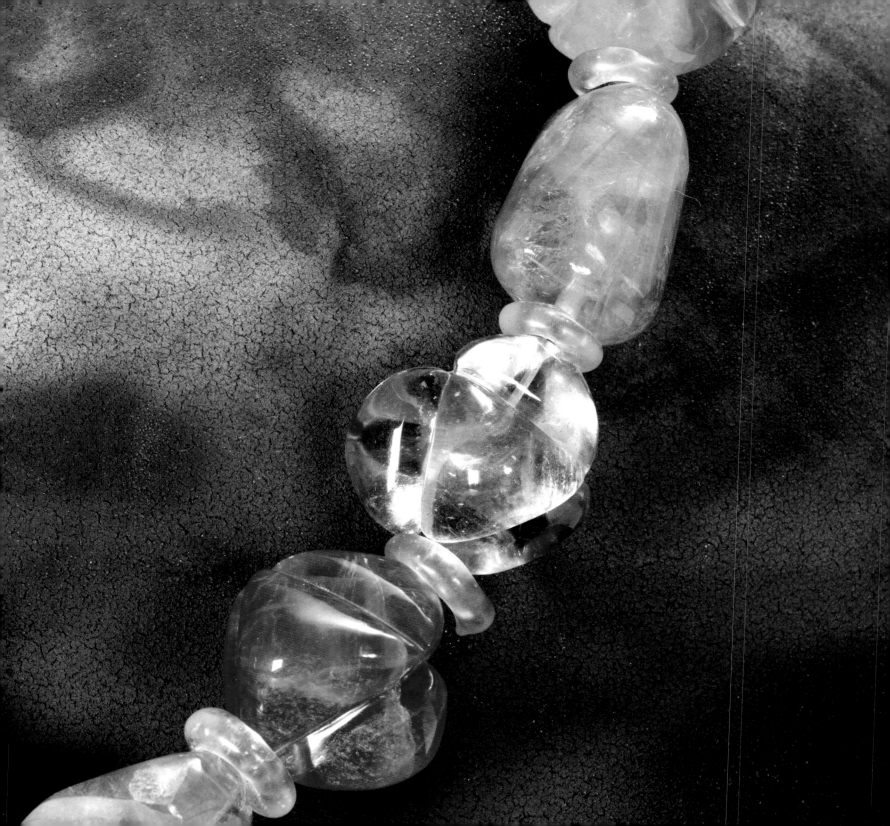

BEADAZZLED
Where Beads & Inspiration Meet

Photographs by WILLIAM L. ALLEN

Penelope Diamanti

BEADAZZLED

TAKOMA PARK, MARYLAND

PHOTOGRAPHY: *William L. Allen*

ART DIRECTION: *Constance H. Phelps*

TEXT AND CAPTIONS: *Penelope Diamanti*

COPY EDITING AND RESEARCH: *Joyce Diamanti*

STYLING: *Constance H. Phelps, Penelope Diamanti, Carol Allen, Kathleen Webber*

MODELING: *Demetra, Joanna Foucheux, Khin, Mallika Noorani, Emily Phelps,*
Jennifer Sammons, Emily Shammas

ADMINISTRATIVE AND RESEARCH ASSISTANCE: *Annie Grybauskas*

ADMINISTRATIVE ASSISTANCE: *Emily Shammas*

INDEXING & EDITING ASSISTANCE: *Pat Diamanti*

PRINTING: *Worzalla*

COVER IMAGE:
GRAZIA ZALFA
Silver Tuareg amulet box from Niger.
African amber, turquoise, Indian silver,
and vinyl heishi.
Box: 87mm

BACK COVER IMAGE:
GRAZIA ZALFA
New look for the ancient technique of drawn
cane beads by David Christensen.
Center bead: 40mm

IMAGE FACING TITLE PAGE:
GRAZIA ZALFA
Close-up of carved fluorite separated by
antique clear glass annular trade beads.
Purple bead: 30mm

IMAGE OPPOSITE:
PENELOPE DIAMANTI
Three necklaces of Afghan lapis and
high-karat Indian gold. Small central
pendant of Lord Ganesh, the "remover of
obstacles." Devotees invoke him to confer
blessings on new ventures.
Pendant: 15mm

Copyright © 2006 Beadazzled, Inc.
SAN: 850-4199
Beadazzled, Inc.
6930 Carroll Ave. #920
Takoma Park, MD 20912

Cataloging-in-Publication Data
Diamanti, Penelope
   Beadazzled, where beads and inspiration meet
   Bibliography
   Includes index
1.   Contemporary Jewelry
   I. Allen, William L. II. Title

Library of Congress Control Number: 2006901633

ISBN 0-9778820-2-0

Printed and bound in the United States.

Measurements in this book are in millimeters,
because that is the standard used in the bead trade.
Each dimension listed is the largest dimension
for the object mentioned.

4

GRAZIA ZALFA
*Treasure necklace of Ethiopian and
North African silver pendants with vintage
charms, found objects, and trade beads.*
Central cross: 50mm

THIS BOOK IS DEDICATED TO ALL THE ARTISTS
who have generously shared their work with you in this volume,
and especially to Grazia Zalfa who, with unbounded imagination,
mastery of diverse techniques, enthusiastic world-wide pursuit of inspiration,
and willingness to cut up just about anything to make jewelry,
has created a kaleidoscopic array of necklaces.

6

Acknowledgements

A true partner in this venture, Bill Allen's enthusiasm,
creativity, and humor have been invaluable
in getting this book out of my head and onto paper.
Connie Phelps' superb design skills and elegance
transformed the raw components into the gem you are holding.
Many other people contributed: My parents, not only gave me life,
but also the love, values, and education to support all that I have accomplished.
My grandmother, Agnes Lovendahl Stewart, whose work is represented herein,
inspired me in more ways than I can list, as did my courageous immigrant grandfather,
John Diamanti, a man of many talents. My sisters, Meli and Pat, have always encouraged me,
and Pat, along with Cas Webber, Deborah McClintock, and Jenni Moore, made it possible
for me to complete this project without hurting our business. Annie Grybauskas' bright
willingness organizational skills, and good taste in music made the job much easier.
— *Penelope Diamanti*

My thanks and admiration to Penny for her vision and Connie for her elegance.
Domo arrigato gozaimas to Kenji Yamaguchi for his continuing and critical advice. To George Bounelis,
my ever-helpful lead guide, and to Bill Reicherts and Clay Burneston, my deep appreciation for getting me
safely through an unfamiliar thicket. To Demetra, Joanna Foucheux, Khin, Mallika Noorani, Emily Phelps,
Jennifer Sammons, and Emily Shammas, thank you for enhancing the beauty of the necklaces with your beauty.
And to my wife, Carol, my gratitude for enduring my total focus on yet another project.
— *William L. Allen*

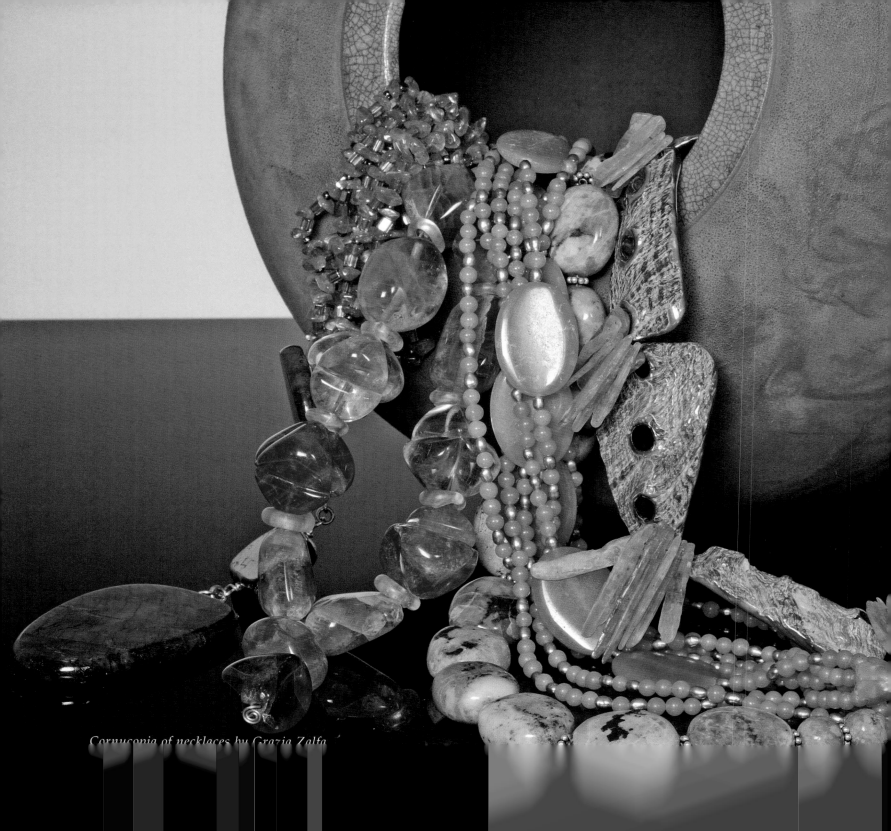

Cornucopia of necklaces by Grazia Zaffa

CONTENTS

INTRODUCTION

nspiration! Literally, the word means the inhalation and exhalation of breath that gives us life. Beyond that definition, however, lives another: "an infusion into the mind or soul" that lights our spiritual, intellectual, and creative fires. When inspiration meets a medium as diverse as beads, magic happens.

I'm often amazed when confident artists from another field encounter beads in our store. Not for them the simple patterns copied from how-to books. They dive right into the deep end, pursuing a vision they are determined to manifest. They blithely disregard the normal stringing methods and conventional functions of clasps or earring parts, seeing instead their potential as design elements or connectors to support their non-traditional beaded structures. Early on, I was tempted to suggest simpler designs, afraid that the complexity of their first project would frustrate them. But I've learned that creativity is fundamentally about problem-solving; about seeing things in a new way and achieving the desired result through novel means. In this sense, creativity applies to all aspects of our lives, from work to relationships, and everyone is creative.

My family celebrated several "official artists," as Julia Cameron calls them. My grandmother, aunt, cousin, and sister all had recognized talents. I couldn't draw and resigned myself to "not being artistic" until I discovered my medium in an African market in my early twenties. Old and ancient beads from Africa, the Middle East, and Europe spread out on rickety tables in Abidjan's markets drew me in with an irresistible force. I spent all the money I earned—teaching English in the Ivory Coast's capital—on beads. I had no idea why I wanted them; I just had to have them! And soon I had to know more about them. It was 1973 and all kinds of stories circulated about the origins of "African Trade Beads," but little hard information. My lifelong research into the history of beads had begun.

Soon, just possessing these treasures was no longer enough—I wanted to wear them. And when people saw me wearing them, they wanted to wear them too. So I stumbled into making beaded jewelry long before the explosion of bead books, bead stores, and special beading materials. I strung my first designs on dental floss and finished them with clasps I made from hardware-store wire. Influenced by ethnic adornment seen on my world travels, I developed a personal style and techniques to support it, gradually earning a reputation—and a living—with my work. It took another twenty years, however, until I finally started to consider myself "an artist." Many of those whose necklaces appear in this book have followed similarly circuitous paths. One of our missions is to open this wonderfully rewarding road to everyone.

Inspiration is about vision, sparks of insight, and the passionate desire to create. Realizing the vision, however, requires disciplined practice, leading to dexterity and eventually virtuosity, in the chosen medium. As the musician endlessly practices scales until her fingers can reproduce on her instrument the melodies in her heart, the beader usually starts with simple patterns, moving on as her skills expand, until she begins solving design challenges in new ways. This book seeks to document the work of leaders in the field and to encourage exploration by novices. It is deliberately not a how-to book. Artists are always on the lookout for inspiration, the breath that fans our creative fires. Students copy to learn, but artists are past the point of literal copying. We hope this book will provide a map of new territory for you to explore in your own way.

Inspiration is the jumping off point into the ocean of our own imaginations. The creative response may be evoked by an unexpected color harmony in nature, a tribal costume, an exotic architectural detail, or the provocative juxtaposition of components of different eras, cultures, or materials. Whatever wakes up our creative instinct ignites our desire to express our own visions. As Grazia Zalfa abundantly demonstrates throughout this book: "…everything around me inspires me. I can look at a tree and see a necklace!" Miachelle DePiano describes experiences many of us share: "There are times I have so many ideas I can't sleep…and spend my nights lying in bed picturing how to put together a new piece."

"Inspiration is about vision and the passionate desire to create. Realizing the vision requires disciplined practice."

Because people have been working with beads for tens of thousands of years, it's unlikely that any design is completely original, but creative people continue to develop distinctive and exciting interpretations. If we have succeeded in our mission, you will be torn between looking at the following pages and running to your own collection of beads to get to work!

Many artists feel that the beads themselves dictate the shape they want to take. Deanna Marie Finocchiaro: "I strongly believe [the designs] grow naturally out of the materials…with a little encouragement on my part." Ellen Benson adds, "As beads travel through many different arrangements in my mind and on the work table, the rules…and taboos that each component imposes on the design become apparent and guide me." Shawn Judge: "I let the piece tell me where it wants to go, and as a result, I rarely undo 'mistakes.' I use them to lead me on journeys into different combinations of color, shape, texture, and movement." Many of us realize that old beads carry energy with their history. Kathlyn Moss: "…because beads are made from the substances of the earth and have passed through many hands, I believe they contain a spiritual element which just naturally finds its way into each piece of jewelry."

Even scientists recognize that beads are deeply linked to what makes us human—and what makes us reach beyond. Beads are among the earliest expressions of artistic creativity and symbolic thinking, which distinguish us from other animals. The first materials used as beads were probably seeds, berries, leaves, and similar materials that have not survived. The oldest beads excavated to date are tiny perforated shells found in southern Africa, dating back 75,000 years. In the "creative explosion" beginning about 40,000 years ago, beads proliferated in Australia, Asia, and Europe as well as Africa. As hunter-gatherers developed new tools and techniques, they used a wider variety of materials to make jewelry, often imbued with symbolism. Animal bones, tusks and teeth, horn and antler connected hunter and prey. Ostrich eggshell, many species of seashells, coral, amber, and soft stones, such as steatite and serpentine were chosen sometimes for their evocative colors and shapes; sometimes just because they were plentiful and/or easy to pierce.

Especially desirable materials were traded from distant sources over routes that would grow into vast networks linking diverse cultures. From earliest times, beads have been connected to our technological inventiveness, our restless urge to explore, and our entrepreneurial spirit.

The more we work with beads the more we care about where they came from. Lynne Merchant: "I like to understand the genesis of the objects I am working with so that I can authentically honor them in my work." My personal mission has been to translate the importance of heirloom beads from the cultures where I find them to the one where I live now, creating necklaces that are beautiful, comfortable, and meaningful.

Self-awareness, another defining factor for humanity, shows up in Paleolithic personal adornment. Anthropologists think that variations in the beaded ornaments of voluptuous female figurines may have indicated group affiliation. An early reader of this text suggested that maybe the ancient carver was motivated by "desire for some hot chick from the next cave." That could certainly be the case, but either way her beads were important enough for him to spend time carving them. Maybe the artist thought the necklaces made her more beautiful, maybe they represented a gift he planned to give her, maybe they identified her as available and from a friendly clan, maybe they conveyed that she was a princess or a priestess. We'll never know for sure, but we do know that throughout millennia of social, economic, political, religious, industrial, and technological revolutions, beads remain important for all the same reasons today.

It may be hard to believe, now that mainstream fashion has embraced our once-funky gear, but when we "flower children" were graduating from college three decades ago, we thought we had to discard our peasant blouses, lovingly-embroidered jeans, and comfortable Birkenstocks. We put away our beaded Indian tunics and our flowing sequined skirts. We

CAROLYN KNIGHT
Vintage Baoule lost-wax cast mask from Ivory Coast. Venetian glass trade beads, coconut shell and clamshell from West Africa see also p. 54-55.
Pendant: 95mm

struggled into "power suits" and pointy, painful shoes as we went to look for work. But we did not give up our beads!

Like the "gaydar" that picks up the subtlest of signals between men seeking each other, our beaded earrings telegraphed an entire set of counter-culture values to kindred spirits, while remaining indecipherable to the uninitiated. When I moved East from California, I found no members of my "tribe" in my government jobs, but when I went to work at National Geographic, I felt at home among world travelers with an appreciation for cultural diversity and art.

"If we have succeeded in our mission with this book you will be torn between looking at the pages and putting it down to run to your own collection of beads and get to work."

Decades passed. Women achieved many political and economic goals. We began to relax and shed the armor of our corporate costumes. We let our hair down, we embraced wearable art, we started our own businesses—and our beads came out of the closet again. In reclaiming our lives and our values we also reconnected with the unseen forces our Stone Age ancestors were trying to contact when they carved those lovely little fertility goddesses.

Understanding those forces is especially important when leaving this life. Archeologists have learned much from the beads people tried to take with them, as in the case of two children buried together on the Ice Age Russian steppe more than 25,000 years ago. Their regal outfits included more than 10,000 beads of mammoth ivory, each requiring an hour to make, for a total of five years of dedicated labor. After nomads began to settle into permanent communities around 12,000 years ago, people developed increasingly sophisticated bead-making techniques. The bow drill, later tipped with diamond chips, made it possible to drill beads of turquoise, lapis lazuli, and harder stones, such as agate, carnelian, and rock crystal. The earliest metal artifacts were beads forged from native copper, followed by beads of bronze and precious gold and silver. People learned to make pottery, and soon were producing ceramic beads of every size and shape. These were succeeded by beads of man-made materials, faience and then—most magnificent bead material of all—glass, which appeared in the form of beads in the 2nd millennium BC in Mesopotamia and the Indus and Nile Valleys. The Egyptians quickly adapted the wondrous new substance to beadmaking, launching a tradition that thrived around the Mediterranean, especially in Venice during the Age of Exploration, and continues to evolve today.

As new materials and technologies emerged, artists invariably appropriated them to make beads. Enameling, cloisonné, ceramic glazes, and latex paints dressed beads in stunning colors. Bakelite and other early plastics, dichroic glass (developed for the space program), and polymer clay and Precious Metal Clay (PMC) increased beadmaking options with entirely new media. Yet ancient techniques for crafting glass and stone beads individually by hand coexist with modern mass production, and beads—new as well as old—still speak to the deepest parts of our human nature, continuing to fuel a passion for beads around the globe.

Clearly beads endure. Inara Knight knows it first hand: "…this passion for beads took me early in life and is still captivating me now, almost 50 years later…It demonstrates the power of beads throughout history; although small, they are very potent!" Candace Cloud McLean agrees: "Beads are magical little pieces of happiness with a hole in them. I don't understand their mesmerizing quality. I just know that I find happiness and creative satisfaction in their presence." We can feel the energy of all the hands these beads have been through. We can imagine all the things they've seen on their travels through time and space. We can relate to the women who wore them. And they serve to connect us—to ourselves and to each other—in an increasingly disconnected world. Sis Morris: "I have made wonderful friends who share my passion for beads. We go on bead fieldtrips together, inspire each other, and collaborate on new projects. Most of all we encourage one another and laugh together."

We hope that what you learn about beads in this book will increase your appreciation of them, and whether you are new to beading or have been long on this path, we hope this book will delight you, expand your horizons, and inspire you to express your own unique vision with these magical materials.

GEMSTONES

Showcasing rocks, minerals & precious stones

CAITO AMOROSE

"Queen's Jewels" of clear quartz crystals on wire. Amorose is "drawn to sparkling, glittering phenomena like twinkling stars." Crystal healers say clear quartz facilitates spiritual growth.

Crystals: 7mm

On a beach in California I once discovered more stones with natural holes than I could carry. As I scurried around collecting them, I thought how fortunate our ancestors would have felt to discover these beautiful hard materials, already perforated and ready to wear! Even rough rocks and smooth pebbles exude a simple elegance. Radiant precious and semiprecious gemstones, difficult to mine, shape, pierce, and polish, were originally worn only by pharaohs, kings, and emperors. Later, high priests and wealthy nobles also claimed the right to adorn themselves with gemstones, swelling the demand for ornaments produced by master craftsmen. Among the many legends about bead materials, the largest body of lore relates to gemstones. Most people know what their birthstone is, and many wear various "lucky" stones. Ancient Vedic astrology links gemstones to the zodiac and prescribes gem remedies for difficult aspects. Books are filled with both ancient and New Age lore concerning specific (and sometimes contradictory) properties: banded agates for courage and strength, amethyst for self-discipline, reducing anger and anxiety or to avoid intoxication, carnelian for healing and motivation, citrine to promote undisturbed sleep, emeralds for love and creativity, garnets for sexual vitality and good fortune, lapis lazuli for wisdom and power, rubies for health, sapphires to attract divine favor, turquoise to protect travelers, avoid the evil eye, and cure headaches. Whether we attach meaning or simply enjoy their infinite color harmonies and varied textures, the gems that follow are sure to inspire.

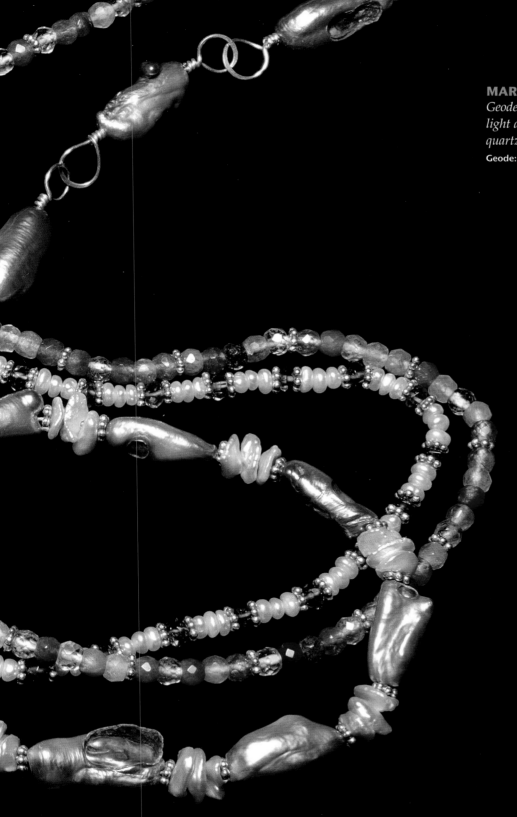

MARY HICKLIN

Geode, cut by Gary Wilson, sparkles and glows with inner light accentuated by pearls, faceted green rutilated quartz, smoky topaz, silver, and glass seed bead fringes.

Geode: 52mm

MARY HICKLIN

Named "Ode to Sping" for green kyanite reminiscent of blades of grass, this work includes pearls, faceted green garnet, Indian granulated vermeil (gold-plated sterling) spacers and seed beads.

Longest blade: 46mm

GRAZIA ZALFA (opposite)

Green kyanite, sprouting like seaweed, connects shells. Zalfa feels "A beautiful design can include beads from many places and be made of humble or exotic materials."

Shells: 60mm

KAT WEST

*Art glass bead by Leah Fairbanks harmonizes with
faceted ametrine, round amethyst, and vermeil.
Heat turns amethyst golden, producing citrine.
Transitional ametrines contain both colors.*

Fairbanks' bead: 57mm

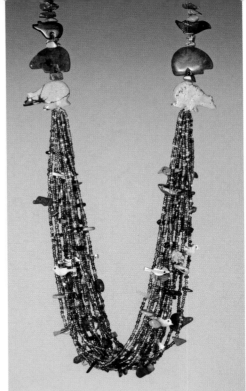

MELISSA DIAMANTI AND ALICE JAMES

Stacked turquoise, pipestone, and jet bear "fetishes" anchor many strands of glass seed beads interspersed with turquoise nuggets, shell, and gemstone birds.

Shell birds: 15mm

GRAZIA ZALFA (opposite)

Treasure trove of turquoise and coral, a combination equally beloved in Asia and the American Southwest. From left: lapis and turquoise (see p. 27), bird "fetishes", Nepalese pendant with turquoise and coral (see p. 76).

Bird: 50mm

CHRISTINE S. GAGNON
*"My work is inspired by the color and shape of
the beads...I love to go to gem and mineral
shows to find my inspiration."* Here turquoise
chips and seed beads frame and support
the cabochon (flat-backed stone).

Clasp: 24mm

GRAZIA ZALFA
*Contemporary Native American pendant
inlaid with dark blue lapis, turquoise, and
purple sugilite. Regal lapis symbolizes power;
to Navajos, turquoise represents the sky god;
rare sugilite might dispel jealousy.*

Pendant: 120mm

GEMSTONES *27*

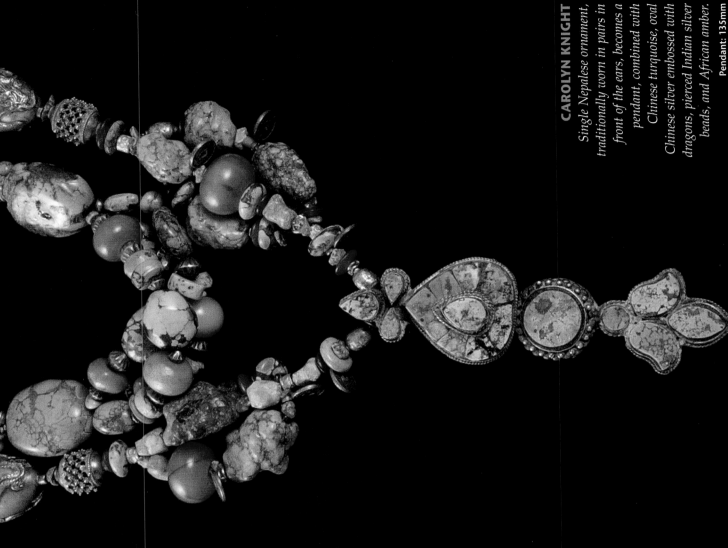

CAROLYN KNIGHT

Single Nepalese ornament, traditionally worn in pairs in front of the ears, becomes a pendant, combined with Chinese turquoise, oval Chinese silver embossed with dragons, pierced Indian silver beads, and African amber.

Pendant: 135mm

GRAZIA ZALFA (opposite)

"Forty-six years ago I bought a necklace, wore it once, didn't like it, so I re-made it. That's how my life-long love of working with beads began." Here large labradorite beads become pendants supported by chips.

Largest bead: 80mm

MARY HICKLIN

This necklace includes "love beads" sent to the artist by friends and strangers from around the country after her studio burned in 2003. Hicklin chose fancy jasper, pink rhodonite, and seed beads to coordinate with the Vesuvianite cabochon cut by Lion's Den and art glass bead by Gail Crossman-Moore (not seen in this photo).

Round beads: 6mm

GRAZIA ZALFA

*Tiny glass "melon beads" and dark jade disks complete
light Chinese jade flowers. Silk cords pass through white
alabaster beads and weave over and under the flowers
to keep them facing forward.*

Largest flower: 35mm

ALEX AND LEE (opposite)

*Famous for their flamboyant bead and fiber creations
in the 70s, one member of this team still works in beads.
The elegant dangles gleam with Balinese granulated
vermeil and rutilated quartz.*

Round center bead: 16mm

MARGO FIELD

Etherial smoky quartz and earthy vintage German glass embellished with seed bead and seed pearl tendrils. Award-winning designer Field teaches beadwork to others "because I feel that everyone has a creative spirit that needs to be nourished."

Center bead: 27mm

PENELOPE DIAMANTI

Guatemalan jade turtle harnessed to a Chinese jade baby bangle. Round jade beads frame elaborate brass buttons drilled to become beads. Rhyolite rondelles, serpentine pendant, and new brass castings of old Indian silver dangles round out the palette.

Bangle: 70mm

BONNIE VOELKER

Web of copper wire supports collar of carnelian chips, olive jade leaves, and glass bead flowers. "I like to work large" states the artist. Details show front and back.

Leaves: 32mm

CHIPITA

Expert colorist, most famous for her earrings, Chipita likes to work small. Her intricate designs of tiny Swarovski crystals, carnelian, and vermeil often include chain.

Dangles: 7mm

GRAZIA ZALFA (opposite)

Rough citrine briolettes and citrine rondelles recall ancient excavated treasures. Warmly glowing citrine is recommended to support progress in business, education, and interpersonal relationships.

Center bead: 30mm

MELISSA DIAMANTI

Versatile two-strand lariat can be worn as choker, long necklace or even belt. Pietersite, dime-shaped pearls, various jaspers, and glass seed beads all contribute earthy tones.

Dangle: 50mm

JEREMY AND CARRI GICKER

*Partners in marriage and art, this couple
specializes in combining stunning stones
with metal. Three necklaces of various
agates mixed with glass and silver.*

Center pendant: 45mm

WALTER FORD (opposite)

*Banded agates echo the delicate lines in
Hill Tribe silver pendant and beads from
Thailand. Milky opal glass rondelles match
agate's bands without eclipsing them.*

Pendant: 63mm

CHRISTINE GAGNON

Mostly self-taught, Gagnon favors bead embroidery and cites Shari Serafini as an inspiring influence. Here she pairs chalk turquoise with olive jade and Czech glass seed beads and leaf dangles.

Centerpiece: 61mm

JANEEN WALKER (opposite)

"Beadwork has become my all consuming passion within the last year!" After teaching high school English and working in corporate risk management, Walker finds being creative liberating and is "most inspired by the people I meet in bead stores, and by the elements of nature." Mossy shades of jade, peridot, serpentine, and green turquoise complement purple amethyst and garnet.

Center stone: 45mm

AFRICA

Inspired by the beads & cultures of Africa

GRAZIA ZALFA

Engraved silver amulet box, fabricated by nomadic Tuareg smiths of Mali and Niger, with diamond-shaped amber often worn in Sahel women's hair. European manufacturers developed the colorful vinyl discs (also called "Heishi") for West African markets where similar beads of black coconut shell and white clamshell were popular.

Amulet box: 87mm

My own story begins here, where I discovered my affinity with beads in the 1970s. Many fellow designers had similar experiences. Elaine Robnett Moore: "My work as an international development consultant in West Africa…was pivotal in my education about the powerful spiritual aspects of indigenous cultures and the way that power is often manifested in jewelry, especially beaded jewelry. Combining the magic of beads and my travel experiences, along with my own African-American heritage, I create wearable art…." Beads made in Africa of bone, shell, and amber (both real and faux), glass beads, and brass ornaments cast by the lost-wax method, flooded our shores along with tons of "trade beads." It took us a while, and a lot of help from researchers like Robert Liu, Peter Francis, Jr., and Jamey Allen, to figure out the ages and origins of the many beads traded to Africa over the centuries. Long before Europeans arrived carnelian beads from India crossed seas and deserts, to reach ancient kingdoms in West Africa. Roman and Islamic glass beads spread south from the Mediterranean. Later Portuguese, French, Dutch, and English traders brought boatloads of beads produced in Venetian and Bohemian glass factories. The latter sent intrepid agents to Africa to discover which beads were most valued, so they could reproduce them in glass. The tide turned in the 1960s, when Africans developed new tastes and began exporting old beads to Americans craving the exotic. Today we are enjoying a resurgence of interest in large, bold, pieces.

GISELLE HECHT
Antique Venetian millefiori (thousand flowers)
mosaic beads, black and white polka dot "eye"
beads, and lampworked "wave" beads mixed with red
Chinese cinnabar, yellow glass, and turquoise.
Cinnabar: 12mm

GRAZIA ZALFA (far right)
Lightbulb-shaped beads, known as
"wedding beads" because drummers traditionally
wear them for African marriage celebrations, are strung
with long bone "hairpipe" and glass eye beads.
Hairpipe: 50mm

AGNES STEWART (above)

*Oval white agates, known as "moonstones" in Africa, traveled across the
Arabian Sea and the Sahara centuries ago. Later, European traders
brought small red "whitehearts," and classic Venetian glass trade beads.
Inlaid ebony bicones and central silver bead add Arabian influences.*

Silver bead: 49mm

AGNES STEWART

Antique brass chain, modeled after Ashanti gold originals, connects treasures from Ivory Coast markets circa 1970: large white "moonstones", rare tabular Venetian glass decorated with both lampworking and mosaic cane slices (detail above), brass bicones from Cameroon, lost-wax-cast brass spirals, pink and green recycled "powder glass" beads made in Ghana, vintage seed beads, and mini chevrons. For style of necklace as it is worn see similar design next page.

Largest white bead: 46mm

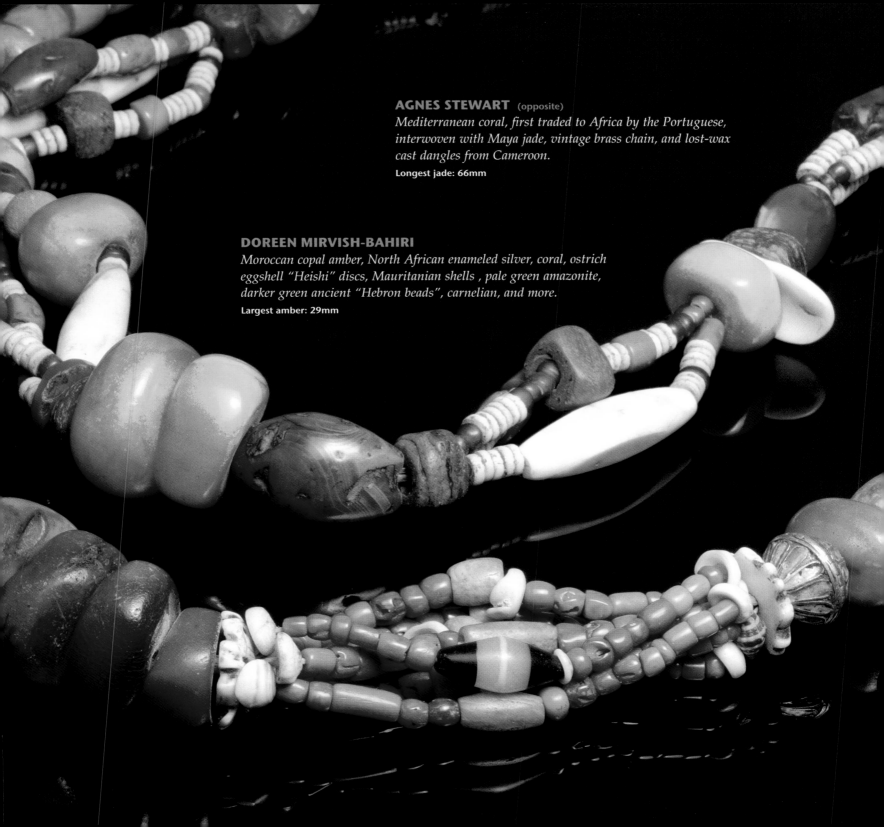

AGNES STEWART (opposite)
Mediterranean coral, first traded to Africa by the Portuguese, interwoven with Maya jade, vintage brass chain, and lost-wax cast dangles from Cameroon.
Longest jade: 66mm

DOREEN MIRVISH-BAHIRI
Moroccan copal amber, North African enameled silver, coral, ostrich eggshell "Heishi" discs, Mauritanian shells , pale green amazonite, darker green ancient "Hebron beads", carnelian, and more.
Largest amber: 29mm

CAROL SAVAGE (opposite)

Old silver collected in Cairo and Istanbul souks includes Yemeni amulet made to hold verses from the Koran. Antique Venetian "feather" beads, clear glass "donuts," and beads from a Kenyan women's co-op complete the design.

Amulet case: 104mm

ELLEN BENSON

Tuareg "crosses", once worn by men and boys, now find favor with women. Named after desert oases in Mali where they originated, the upper one is called Iferouane: the lower, from Zinder, portrays both circle and phallic designs serving as a fertility symbol for both sexes. Ebony, glass and silver beads.

Lower pendant: 103mm

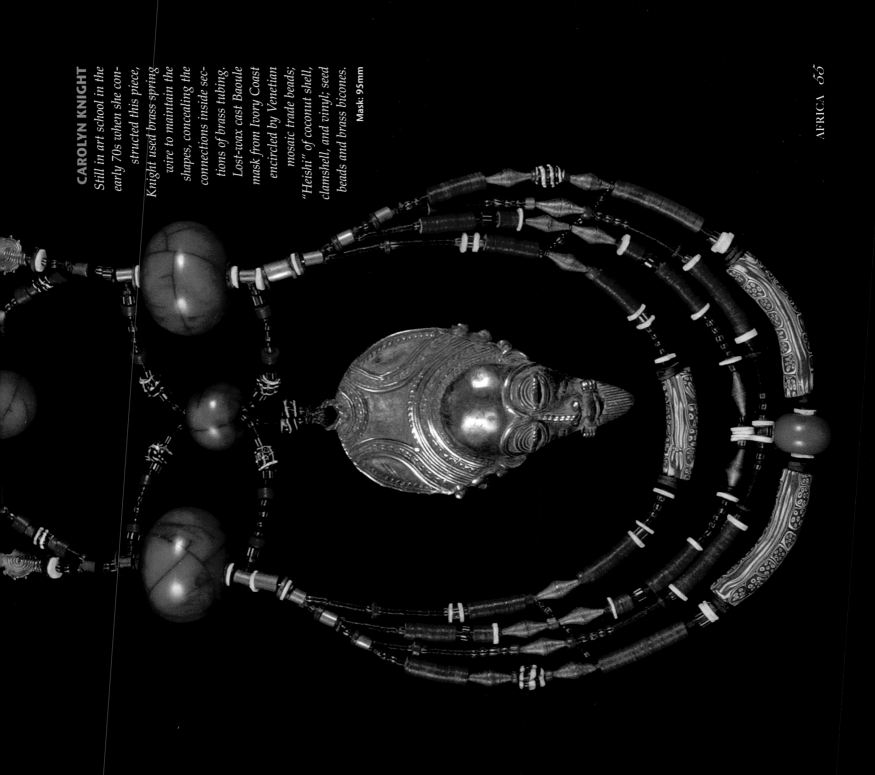

CAROLYN KNIGHT
Still in art school in the early 70s when she con-structed this piece, Knight used brass spring wire to maintain the shapes, concealing the connections inside sec-tions of brass tubing. Lost-wax cast Baoule mask from Ivory Coast encircled by Venetian mosaic trade beads; "Heishi" of coconut shell, clamshell, and vinyl; seed beads and brass bicones.
Mask: 95mm

AGNES STEWART

Portuguese traders brought coral to West Africa where the Kingdom of Benin adopted it as court regalia. Extremely rare, long pieces rest on Venetian glass bicones called "King Beads" because of their importance to Ashanti royalty. African amber and brass bicones from Cameroon tie it together.

Longest coral: 45mm

GRAZIA ZALFA (opposite)

Evocative of Berber designs, this necklace of old silver traded from Yemen, coral, shell, and old coins, also contain modern interlopers: Fimo beads disguised as large coral beads! One seeming to be "repaired" with chain, mimics real coral and amber beads carefully mended with wire because they are irreplaceable.

Center bead: 40mm

PENELOPE DIAMANTI

Left: Detail of Tom Boylan's borosilicate glass bead and Mauritanian amber from an unseen part of necklace at right. Tom Boylan's "feather" bead connects two ambers. Tassels, designed for color, contain a mix of glass and stone beads from Africa, Europe and Asia.

Feather bead: 45mm

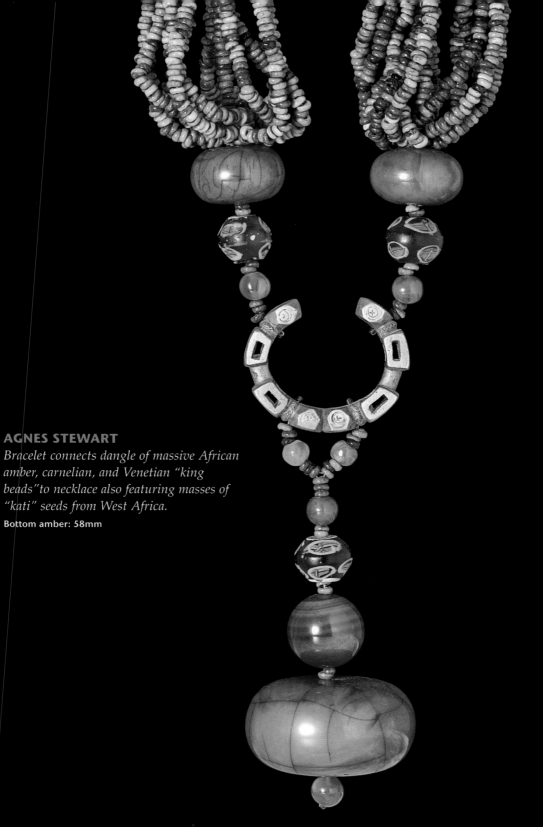

AGNES STEWART

Bracelet connects dangle of massive African amber, carnelian, and Venetian "king beads" to necklace also featuring masses of "kati" seeds from West Africa.

Bottom amber: 58mm

CAROLYN KNIGHT

African amber beads orbit within rings of antique Venetian glass trade beads, black coconut shell, white clamshell, seed beads, and brass. Spring wire.

Largest amber: 38mm

GRAZIA ZALFA

Three regal necklaces. Inner strand: mixed African amber with Indian silver. Middle strand: Venetian "chevrons"— layered cane beads, shaped in a mold, drawn, cut, and ground to reveal the interior pattern at the ends—are highly prized in West Africa and the Americas. Outer strand: Glass beads with lost-wax gold-plated discs modeled after pure Ashanti royal gold ornaments.

Round disc with spider design: 70mm

ELLEN BENSON

Multiple strands, carefully graduated by color and size,
announce one of Benson's most recognizable styles.
Central brass pendant from Ethiopia.

Pendant: 55mm

PHYLLIS ALDRIDGE WOODS

Three strands of ancient agates from Cambay, India traded
to Africa before the Europeans arrived are strung
with gold-plated brass beads from Kenya and Nigeria.

Center white bead: 38mm

AGNES STEWART

Cobalt blue annular beads, commonly known as "Dogon donuts" for the Malian people who favor them, move freely between larger clear glass European trade beads. Lariat design works well as choker with long tassels, as longer necklace with short tassels, or even as a belt.

Largest clear glass bead: 24mm

SHAWN JUDGE

"Improvisation is key in my designs.... My work explores inner complexities... the twists and turns of knotting representing life's journey...." Triangular *"wedding beads" from Mali, old and new lampworked beads, pressed glass, and a stone disc form a wearable sculpture.*

Long black "hairpipe": 57mm

MELISSA DIAMANTI

*African amber, striped oval "watermelon" beads,
carnelian, amazonite, and more radiate from choker of
apple coral and turquoise.*

Diamond amber: 30mm

GRAZIA ZALFA

Cascade of coiled brass dangles spills from brass cone. Perfect yellow and green "king beads" (preferred by Ghanaian royalty) were made in Venice for the African trade.

Brass cone: 160mm

ASIA

Infused with Asian influences & components

GRAZIA ZALFA

GRAZIA ZALFA

Tibetan earrings, used as pendants flank Nepalese silver centerpiece. Old carnelian and Chinese turquoise.

Centerpiece: 80mm

The varied bead traditions of this vast continent could fill volumes. From India come ancient carnelian beads, tiny glass "trade-wind beads," sacred rudraksha seeds, and exquisite silver and gold pendants, beads, and findings. The Naga wear multi-strand masses of small glass beads with brass and bone ornaments. In Gujarat and Rajasthan glass beads and cowrie shells embellish colorful textiles. Workshops in Varanasi and near Agra use ancient techniques to make inexpensive wound and drawn glass beads for world markets. Peoples of Tibet and Nepal prize coral as symbolizing fire, turquoise as the sky, and amber as the earth, along with mysterious dZi beads. Indonesia is famed for ancient glass Jatim beads and granulated silver beads crafted by Bali's master silversmiths. From Japan come ojime and netsuke, adapted as striking beads. China has long exported cloisonné, porcelain, jade, and carved wood and bone beads. "Rough," the lapidary term for uncut stone, travels to Hong Kong from all over Asia, Africa, Australia, and the Americas to be cut in an ever-increasing array of shapes and drilled for beads. Within the past few years, China has also emerged as a glass beadmaking powerhouse, competing with Swarovski crystals, Venetian mosaic and foil beads, and Indian lampworked beads. Design influences from Asia, many imbued with spiritual symbolism, are as varied as Asian materials. Yoga's increasing popularity in the west has opened new markets for jewelry depicting Hindu deities, reflecting chakra colors and symbols, and conveying Ayurvedic healing properties associated with precious stones.

AMY KAHN RUSSELL

Artist and successful entrepreneur, Russell studied fine arts in Texas, Louisiana, and England. To explain her diverse palette and influences, she says: "I relate to everything." Branch coral flows with turquoise. Jeweled box pendant opens.

Pendant: 54mm

SHERYL STEPHENS

Decorative as well as structural,
spacer bars and three-to-one cones maintain
distance between strands to create a feeling
of mass, even with delicate beads.

Pendant: 40mm

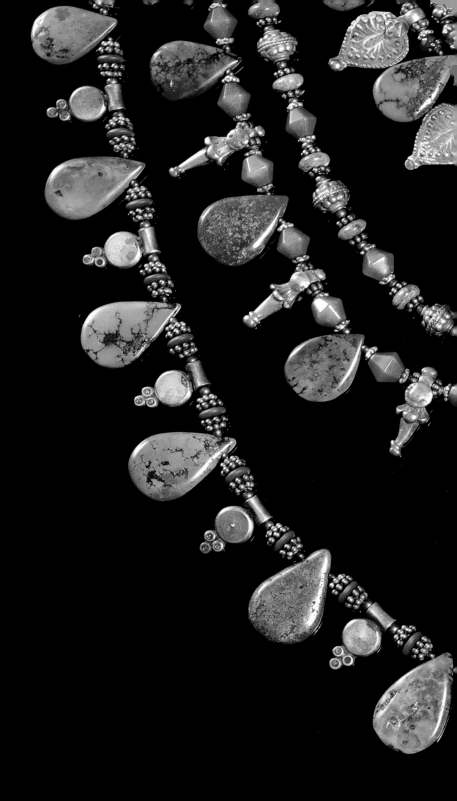

SUSAN GREEN

*Goddess Durga, "destroyer of demons" and consort of
Shiva, rides her lion across temple-shaped pendant. Green
searches markets and bazaars for the finest materials.
Indian silver and brass with Chinese turquoise.*

Durga pendant: 30mm

GRAZIA ZALFA (opposite)

Carnelian and graceful curling fire-gilded imagery, representing stylized animals and birds, adorn traditional Turkmen heart-shaped pendant from Central Asia. Worn on the back, these ornaments comprise only a small part of these nomaic women's finery. Protective hand amulets are popular from Morocco to Israel and beyond.

Heart pendant: 90mm

SUSAN GREEN

Evoking Naga necklaces of India with colors and shape, Green creates a statement with massed strands of small beads and dangles. Irregularity of the seed beads shows their age and hand-made origins.

Brass triangles: 14mm

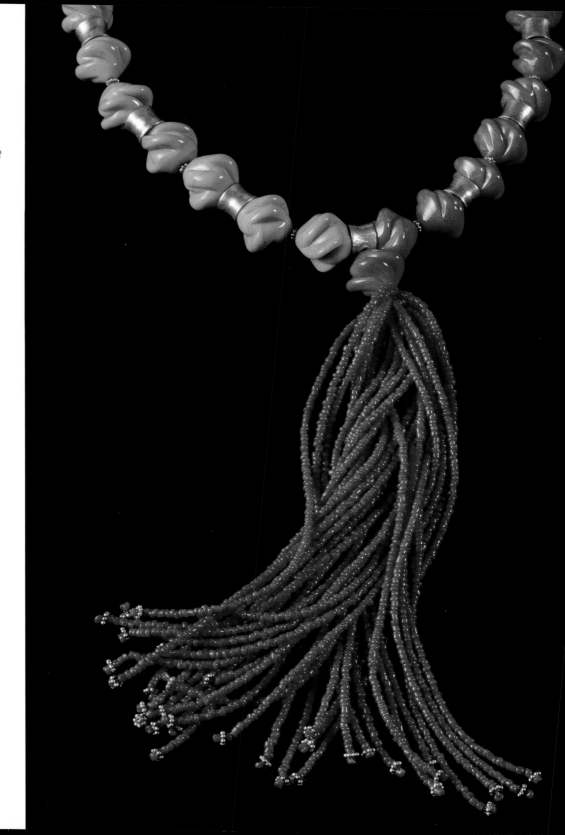

GRAZIA ZALFA

Nepalese pendant of coral and turquoise, with stone nuggets and Chinese carved beads. Prized in China, Mongolia, and Tibet for its ability to protect wearers from evil, turquoise was also pulverized and added to traditional Asian medicines.

Pendant: 110mm

GRAZIA ZALFA

Seed bead tassels flow from vintage glass beads. Whether in stone or glass, these complimentary colors fascinate jewelers around the world.

Tassels: 180mm

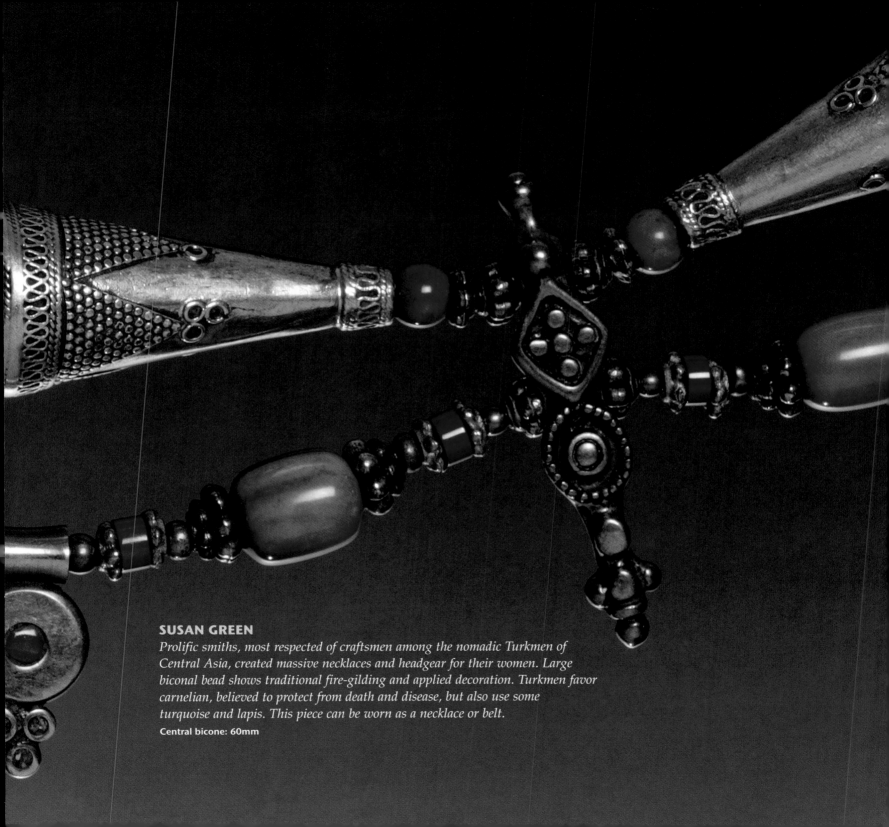

SUSAN GREEN

Prolific smiths, most respected of craftsmen among the nomadic Turkmen of Central Asia, created massive necklaces and headgear for their women. Large biconal bead shows traditional fire-gilding and applied decoration. Turkmen favor carnelian, believed to protect from death and disease, but also use some turquoise and lapis. This piece can be worn as a necklace or belt.

Central bicone: 60mm

DEANNA MARIE FINOCCHIARO

Ginko leaves, associated with healing, longevity, and harmony, appear here as small castings and larger mesh replicas. Cascading from a beaded torque with contemporary art glass beads, the leaves mix with mottled rhyolite, transparent prehnite, and pearls. Detail at left shows secure and intricate finishing that characterizes professional work.

Mesh leaf: 37mm

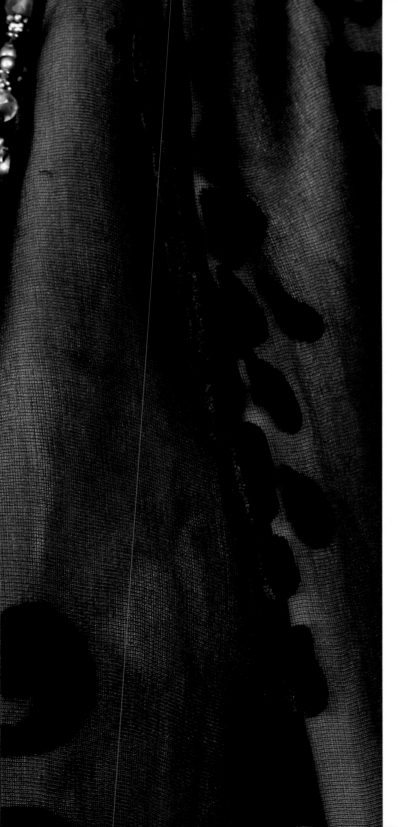

GRAZIA ZALFA

New Zealand style jade carvings. Center pendant depicts miniature of a Maori weapon called "mere". Usually about 16" long, the spatula-shaped club also served as a symbol of rank and became the warrior's most prized possession.
"Mere" pendant: 105mm

SUSAN GREEN

Body contact with stamped deity amulets (especially popular in Rajasthan and Gujarat, India) serves as passive form of worship and indicates the wearer's commitment. This one shows Bhairava, holding a trident that identifies him as a form of Shiva, accompanied by dog (behind his leg).
Faceted prehnite and Indian silver.
Pendant: 66mm

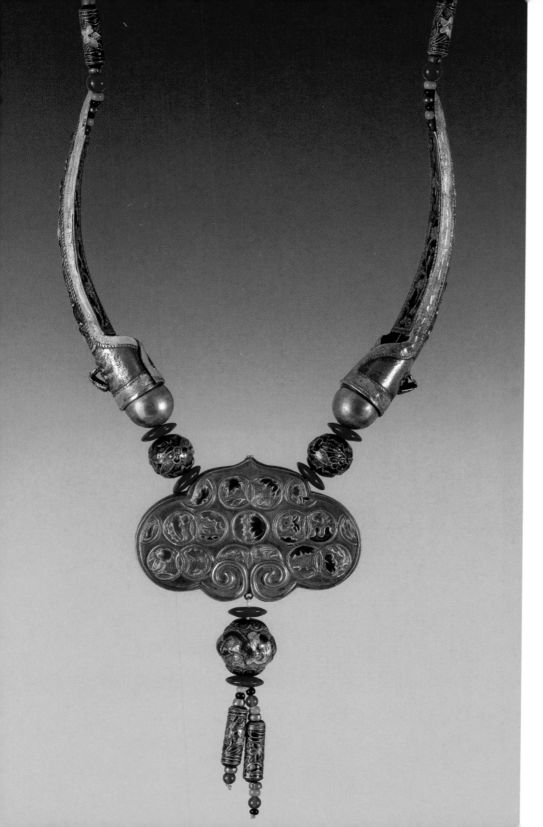

PENELOPE DIAMANTI (left)

Adjustable flaps at their base and ventilated underside mark these Mandarin fingernail protectors as authentic. Shaped like hollow claws and most famously worn by women of China's Qing dynasty, they now neatly encircle a neck. Stylized enamel lock and round beads with carnelian and glass.

Fingernail protectors: 105mm

AMY KAHN RUSSELL

Sometimes called unicorns, the mythical Chinese "qilin" boasts a dragon's head bearing at least one horn. The body of a deer, hooves of a horse, and tail of a lion complete the picture. The young male rider wears the robe of a successful examination candidate. Qing dynasty women hoping for intelligent and industrious male offspring commissioned these popular ornaments.

Qilin including bells: 153mm

AMY KAHN RUSSELL

Russell spent three years in Hong Kong "soaking up Asian culture" and collecting beads and related art. Amulets and talismans surround a central symbolic lock traditionally used to protect children, especially sons, from evil spirits by "locking them to the earth."

Lock: 49mm

SUSAN GREEN

Antique seal becomes a pendant strung with Chinese turquoise, Indian silver, and heavy Nepalese brass beads. All turquoise becomes greener with exposure to body oils, but even new Chinese stones appear greener than most American turquoise because of the greater proportion of iron in their composition. Copper produces the sky blue color associated with Navajo and Persian examples. Turquoise has been revered by ancient Egyptians and Persians, Incas and Aztecs, Chinese, Mongolians, and Tibetans, and is still employed in Navajo ceremonies.

Seal: 55mm

ELLEN BENSON

Cords wrapped with glass beads pass through silver pendant from Afghanistan and terminate in "Russian blue" beads traded in Africa as well as Alaska and the American Northwest coast. Hill Tribe silver beads from Thailand.

Pendant: 50mm

ELLEN BENSON

Small glass beads and whitehearts wrap the cord suspending pendants from Kazakhstan in one of Benson's signature styles. Curator of several shows at the Bead Museum in Washington, DC, Benson considers the history each component brings to her designs along with its color, shape and texture.

Central pendant: 23mm

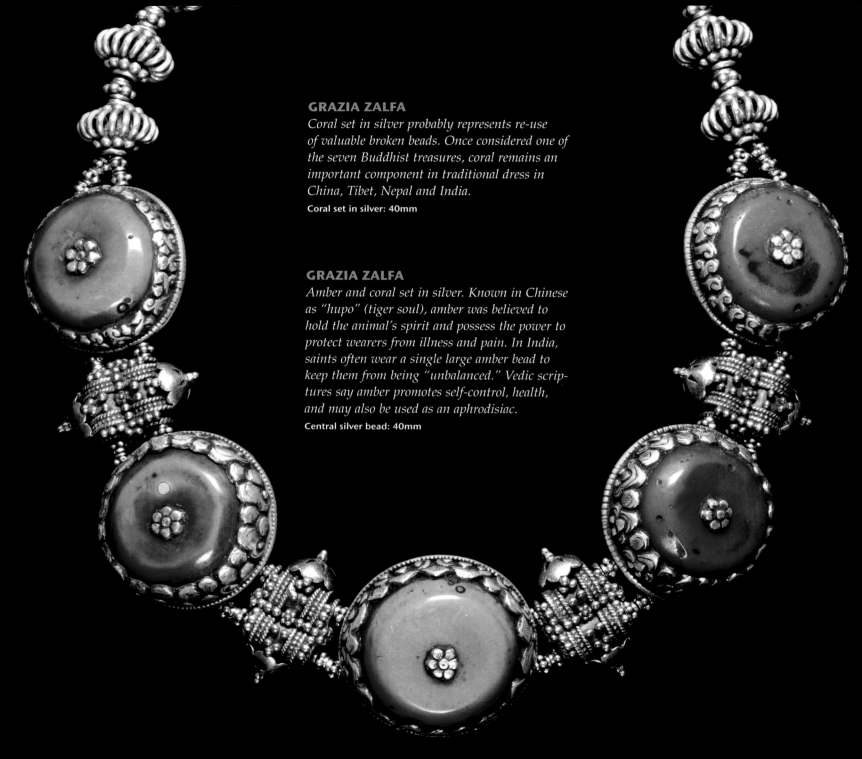

GRAZIA ZALFA

Coral set in silver probably represents re-use of valuable broken beads. Once considered one of the seven Buddhist treasures, coral remains an important component in traditional dress in China, Tibet, Nepal and India.

Coral set in silver: 40mm

GRAZIA ZALFA

Amber and coral set in silver. Known in Chinese as "hupo" (tiger soul), amber was believed to hold the animal's spirit and possess the power to protect wearers from illness and pain. In India, saints often wear a single large amber bead to keep them from being "unbalanced." Vedic scriptures say amber promotes self-control, health, and may also be used as an aphrodisiac.

Central silver bead: 40mm

GRETCHEN SHIELDS

Silver pendant with central lotus motif and animal imagery. Two capped dark brown and cream dZi bead reproductions start the second strand and two small oval dZi appear on the first strand. Related to ancient etched agates and even older naturally-banded stones, dZi have a fascinating history in Tibet.

Pendant: 105mm

KELLY J. ANGELEY

Butterflies and dragonflies of Hill Tribe silver with turquoise and Swarovski crystals. Of the eight groups living in remote hills of northern Thailand, the Karen and Akha are especially known for their silver. Angeley says beading is "the most fun way to use math that I have discovered!" She also finds stringing "meditative... my Bead Zen."

Big butterfly: 56mm

AMY KAHN RUSSELL

Tasseled necklaces of Chinese wood, bone, carnelian, and silver beads. Russell designs bold as well as more delicate styles, using an ever-changing array of natural materials, to appeal to diverse customers.

Bone ring at bottom: 34mm

AMY KAHN RUSSELL

Strands of pearls, carnelian, coral, and light green peridot flow from carved bone frog bead. Bone, carnelian, coral, and olive jade with silver complete the design. Distinctive clasps add value to one-of-a-kind and limited edition designs.

Clasp: 27mm

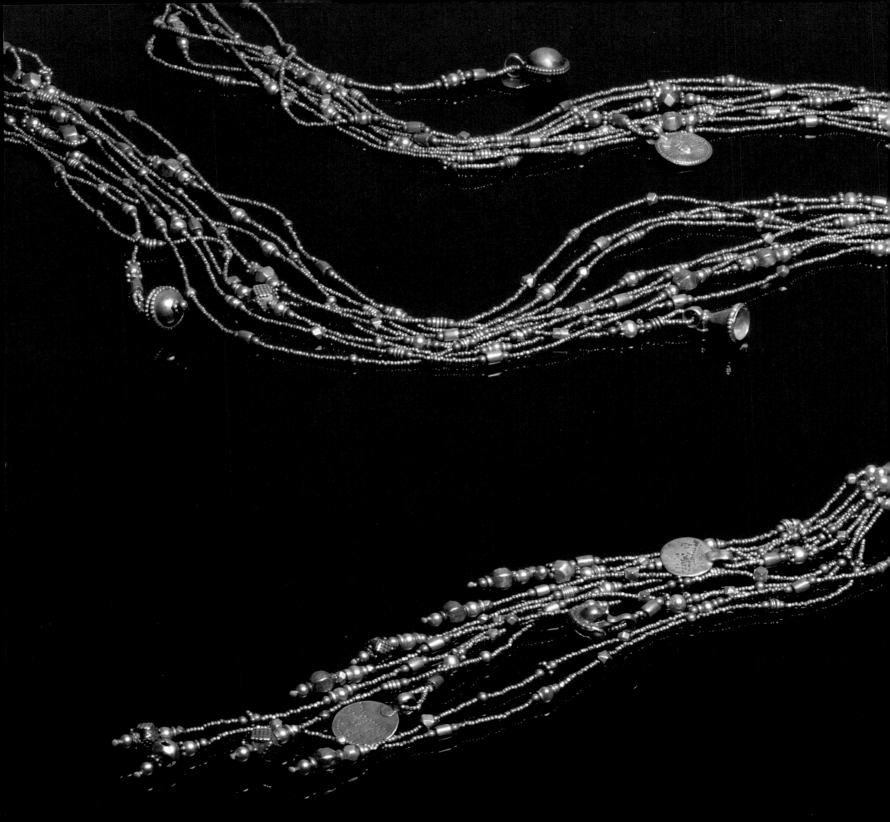

LUCIA ANTONELLI

One of the luminaries of the beaded jewelry renaissance of the 1970s, Antonelli continues to design exotic necklaces using fine materials. Tiny metal beads scavenged from damaged vintage beaded purses add to the subtle metallic sheen of antique Indian silver.

Tiniest beads: 1mm!

NATURE
Exploring wood, bone, shell, pearls, coral & other organics

BONNIE VOELKER

*Nature's bounty: wood, shells
from the Philippines, spiky
sea urchin spines, patterned
batik bone from Kenya,
coral, and small natural and
dyed bone strands.*
Sea Urchin spine: 65mm

Communing with nature energizes our creative souls. Colors, textures, scents, and sounds combine to clear the mind, relax the body, and open the heart. Flowers inspire many designs in other chapters, but here we focus on work composed of organic materials—parts and products of plants and animals. The sea yields shells, fish vertebrae, precious coral, and lustrous pearls. Advances in pearl culture have produced a vast array of nontraditional shapes and colors that have inspired some of this chapter's most exuberant designs. Amber, though often washed up on shorelines, is the petrified sap of ancient conifers. Highly valued amber from around the Baltic Sea in northern Europe was carried south over extensive trade routes to the Mediterranean basin and beyond long before Roman times. In the Americas, Indians trekked from the Pacific to the arid Southwest carrying shells prized by pre-Columbian jewelers. Though trade and transport are easier and faster today, the following pages show that we still treat amber, coral, and shells as precious. The body adornment traditions of Africa and Nepal combine amber and coral with powerful pendants of teeth, bone, horn, and claws, symbolically linking hunters and their prey. Was it a past life as a hunter that attached me to a Rwandan crocodile tooth that I wore through high school? It meant so much to me I asked my dentist to repair it when it broke! Our journeys into nature invariably bring nature back into our work symbolically and energetically. Kathleen Williams weaves twigs and other found objects into her powerful wearable art.

KATHLYN MOSS

"This necklace (titled Volcano Lei) was inspired by visits to Kilauea Volcano in Hawaii." Composed of vintage coral beads and carved red cinnabar with silver caps. Rondelles sprouting seed bead fringe separate the coral beads.

Cinnabar: 15mm

ELAINE ROBNETT MOORE (opposite)

"Africa" reminds Moore of a marketplace, bustling with color and texture. Antique Venetian mosaic and lampworked trade beads interspersed with silver and Egyptian scarabs snake through a horn disc to form an adjustable necklace or belt.

Horn disc: 100mm

KATHLEEN P. MANNING

Double row of abalone shell tabs form a shimmering collar fit for a mermaid. The necklace is reversible, the other side showing more iridescent colors. Manning, who teaches beading at Beadazzled, "can't remember not being interested in beads" and is "amazed by what our students and customers create. They are a great influence and inspiration!"

Shells: 50mm

ANA LIVINGSTON

Kinetic collar of mother-of-pearl, glass bugle and seed beads with silver. Because Livingston used stringing material with some body the lightweight mini strands move with the wearer.

Mother-of-pearl: 50mm

JAMIE CLOUD EAKIN (opposite)

Teacher, author, and "perpetual student of her craft," Eakin accents necklace of shells and mother-of-pearl with rutilated quartz and sea urchin spines.

Flower shell at bottom: 45mm

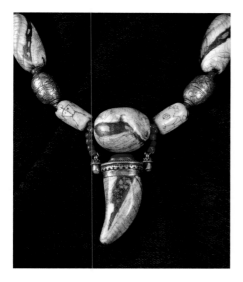

GRAZIA ZALFA

Nepalese carved shell inlaid with turquoise and coral. Designs on cylindrical beads show Naga imagery from India.

Tooth-shaped pendant: 70mm

ELAINE ROBNETT MOORE

"Golden Sands" recalls a Caribbean beach. White shells complement bronze pearls, called "dancers" because their off-center holes create movement. President of the Bead Society of Greater Washington, Moore also teaches jewelry-making and micro-business development.

White shells: 100mm

GRAZIA ZALFA (opposite)

Choker of bamboo coral features Nepalese silver bead set with coral. To Tibetans and Nepalese, good red coral is precious, even outranking gold in desirability. Artisans in Calcutta shape beads from coral originating in the China, Andaman, and Mediterranean Seas.

Silver Bead: 45mm

GRAZIA ZALFA

Italian branch coral forms tassels and suspends the shell from a collar of Nepalese and Philippine shell. Orange glass beads from Nepal mimic coral. In many cultures, poorer residents will accept glass substitutes for precious gems, rather than do without ceremonial jewelry. In China, coral is associated with longevity. In India and Tibet it is believed to stop bleeding.

Coral tassels: 180mm

ELAINE ROBNETT MOORE

*"Fire Dreams"gleams with garnets, red vintage glass and golden amber nuggets.
"This necklace can be worn 14 different ways. Many of those who adopt my
creations say they help satisfy a yearning for a greater sense of connectedness to
the often unexplainable and mysterious energy of the universe," says Moore.*
Rectangular red glass: 10mm

KAT WEST

"I believe that beads transcend mere ornamentation....All that is elemental in beads corresponds to what is elemental within us.... Of everything I have pursued in my many lives, I know that I will bead as long as I am able." Transmitting the artist's sentiments about beading, timeless raku face by Rama wears a headdress of freshwater pearls, seed beads, and Swarovski crystals. Detail above shows hidden clasp with decorative counterweight.

Face: 55mm

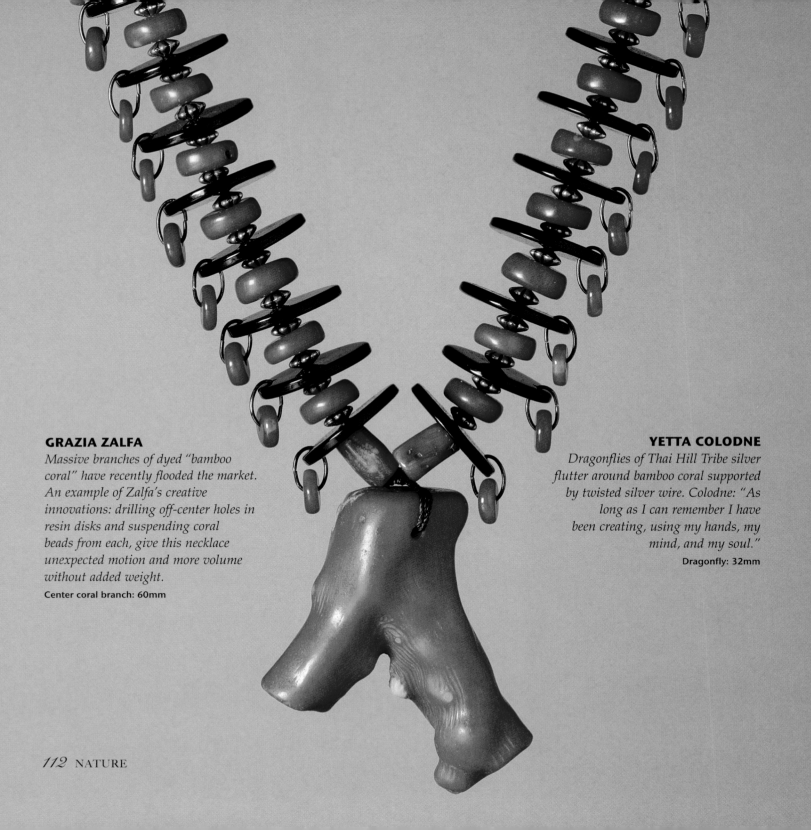

GRAZIA ZALFA

Massive branches of dyed "bamboo coral" have recently flooded the market. An example of Zalfa's creative innovations: drilling off-center holes in resin disks and suspending coral beads from each, give this necklace unexpected motion and more volume without added weight.

Center coral branch: 60mm

YETTA COLODNE

Dragonflies of Thai Hill Tribe silver flutter around bamboo coral supported by twisted silver wire. Colodne: "As long as I can remember I have been creating, using my hands, my mind, and my soul."

Dragonfly: 32mm

GRAZIA ZALFA

*Seed pearls on wire spiral outward like galaxies
in the night sky, showing yet another innovative way
to add visually stimulating dimension to a necklace,
without increasing weight.*

Seed pearls: 4mm

CAITO AMOROSE

*Daisies of stick pearls burst into bloom! The most
creative designers think outside the box, and most
agree that if we listen, the beads will tell us what they
want to be. Amorose knows: "Every bead, just as
every person, presents endless possibilities."*

Stick pearls: 23mm

SHAWN JUDGE
*Organically spreading web of cowrie shells, bone,
and glass seed beads decorates a backdrop of large shells
called "hippo teeth" by the African traders who sell them.
Judge explains her methods: "Knotting techniques…
are stepping stones to move beyond symmetrical
compositions, to angles and curves that lie on
different areas of the neck and breast."*
Polka dot disc: 20mm

GRAZIA ZALFA

Radiating shamanic power, this collar employs multiple rows of small bone beads to link old ivory masks, dark bone faces and Ethiopian bone pendants.

Longest bone pendant: 90mm

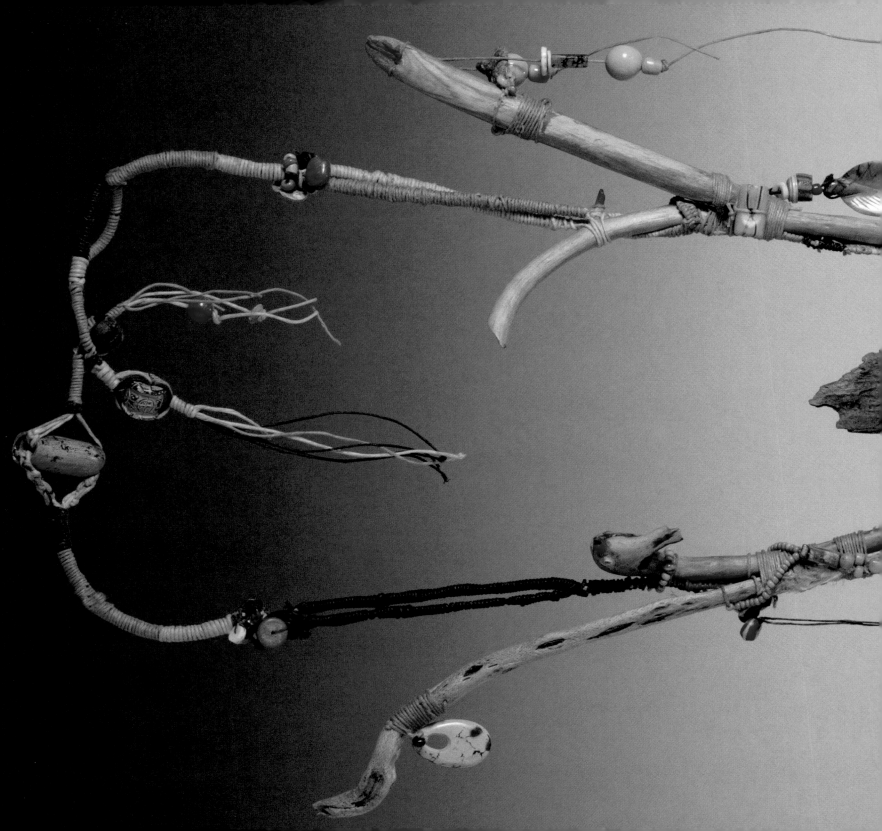

KATHLEEN WILLIAMS

Full of mystery and myriad intriguing visual details, Williams' wearable sculpture "Pale Face" incorporates a raku face, driftwood, trade beads, feathers, shells, and stones, all wrapped with cords. Williams recalls: "His identity was hard to discover as he drifted between being the sphinx, who lives in the woods and the wood itself. But as I added the horse's head and the long curved pieces, it became quite clear that he could be worn and was a warrior from the woods."

Face: 50mm

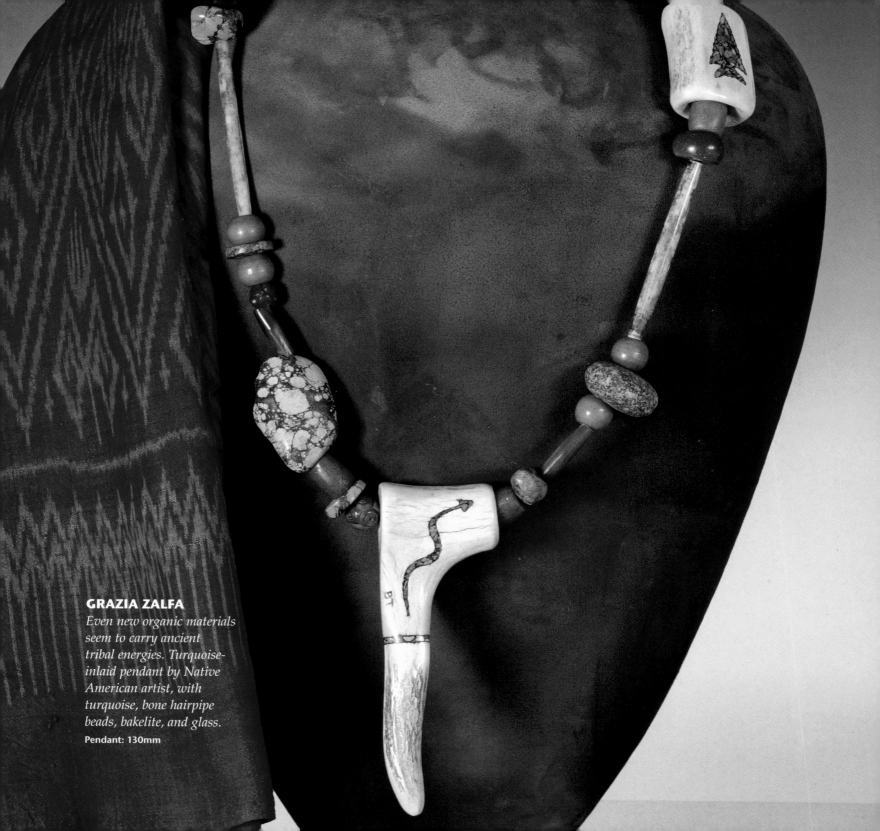

GRAZIA ZALFA

Even new organic materials seem to carry ancient tribal energies. Turquoise-inlaid pendant by Native American artist, with turquoise, bone hairpipe beads, bakelite, and glass.

Pendant: 130mm

TAMMI KINGERY

*The power of nature shines in this collar
of shell tusks and vintage trade beads. The designer's equally
powerful story: "In the early 90s…a family friend told me I should visit
a bead store! Since I have been hearing impaired since birth, I did not
even know what a bead was. I had never heard the word before."
After taking a class "I noticed my creativity and innovation start to grow.
I felt wonderful when my friends started telling me how beautiful
my jewelry was….This addiction has changed my world.
I left the corporate world as a data entry employee,
and am now the manager of a bead store."*

Longest "tusk": 40mm

MICHELLE MEYER (opposite)

Named "Earth and Sea," this necklace features "a fossilized sand dollar from Madagascar beaded with delicas and embellished with shell discs and gold seed beads. I love the feeling of working with something so ancient, it seemed to take shape on it's own...."

Sand dollar: 55mm

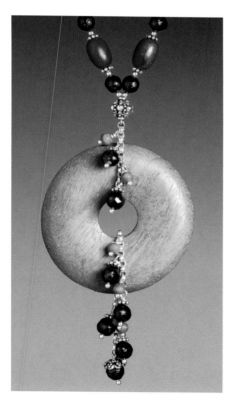

DOTSIE MACK

Wooden "donut" elevated to gem status by Mack's meticulous wire and chain work.

Donut: 49mm

JANE THORNLEY

"The Shaman's Dance is a piece I conjured after a trip to Santa Fe.... This piece honors all shamans by incorporating bits of power images." Wood, amber, shell, dZi replica, tiger's-eye, jasper, silver, copper, and bone.

Largest amber: 17mm

HELGA GROBEL

A clay artist since the early 60s, Grobel focuses on raku because it "combines earth, air, and fire to produce many interesting textures and finishes that are difficult to predict." Needleweaving ties raku beads together with shells, turkey feathers and trade beads from Grobel's collection.

Longest feather: 84mm

HELGA GROBEL

Juxtaposing hard and soft, Grobel alternates raku twisted shapes with turkey feathers. Describing her process: "I just gather beads and all other components and yarns around me…and let it evolve. This method works well for me because I enjoy the element of surprise."

Center raku spike: 75mm

FIBER
Featuring macramé, crochet, needleweaving & more

KRIS BUCHANAN

Shining out from an art glass bead by Nanette Young-Greiner, rays of beads and knotted cord give this piece its name: "Sunny Day."

Center bead: 37mm

*W*hile clothing may have appeared as early as beads, it probably consisted of hides and furs. Fiber arts emerged in the creative explosion, when people first twisted fibers together 30,000 to 20,000 years ago, as evidenced by a Paleolithic figurine sporting a string skirt. The earliest trace of weaving dates to the same period. Only around 7000 BC, however, after farming provided adequate plant and animal fibers and complex looms were developed, did Neolithic artisans begin to systematically produce textiles. The fiber and bead arts are closely allied. Cultures with strong textile traditions—India, Thailand, and Indonesia; Peru and Guatemala; China, Central Asia, and the Himalayan region—also have a rich bead heritage. Similarly, avid bead collectors often love related textiles. Beads complement textiles in both traditional and contemporary clothing and home furnishings. Here we explore creative ways in which jewelry designers employ textile techniques, such as netting, crochet, knitting, macramé, braiding, weaving, tassels, and fringe, to enhance the texture and change the shape of necklaces. Through classes and books, Helen Banes has shared her needleweaving techniques with students across the country, inspiring them to expand their beading repertoire. Fellow author Diane Fitzgerald combines beads and fiber to evoke coiling organic tendrils, while Kristine Buchanan makes magic mixing micro-macramé and beads. Susan Green's trademark technique uses ornamental braid to bind and support her rich multistrand necklaces.

KRIS BUCHANAN (opposite)

"Leafy Garden" showcases polymer clay oval bead and small leaves by Klew with Czech glass flowers. Buchanan prefers freeform micro-macramé and points out that hers is not "the big old plant hanger and owl macramé of the 70s, but small intricate sophisticated macramé for the new millennium."

Center bead: 46mm

KRIS BUCHANAN

An artist for over 40 years, Buchanan feels: "my beadwork is a compilation of all I have learned." Cast copper dangles mingle with coral and stone. Fibers secure hand-decorated bone disc to stone donut and create petals for "Stone Flower."

Clasp: 19mm

GRAZIA ZALFA

Like armor from a Star Wars costume, glass daggers emerge from a collar of overlapping mother-of-pearl buttons. Metallic wire crochet holds it all together.

Buttons: 10mm

SUSAN GREEN

From a fiber-wrapped collar, multiple tiers of glass and stone dangles cascade into an elegant tapered point. Always dramatic, and designed to move with the body, Green's necklaces are also comfortable to wear.

Black bicones: 13mm

GRAZIA ZALFA

Like the bark of a tree or the coat of a magical animal, hundreds of overlapping flat wooden beads cover a crochet bib. Zalfa has collected magazines and books and traveled the world visiting shows and museums in search of inspiration; now she inspires others.

Flat wooden beads: 40mm long

KRIS BUCHANAN

Fused dichroic glass focal bead by Charity Heroux rests on richly beaded knotwork. Buchanan incorporates art glass beads by well-known, and emerging artists "to help promote their work."

Focal bead: 67mm

KRIS BUCHANAN

Glass flounder and red bubble beads by John Rizzi with shells and fiber. Buchanan describes her work: "My pieces are complex, abstract, and asymmetrical, and take many hours to complete, which puts my mind in a place that I love."

Fish: 65mm

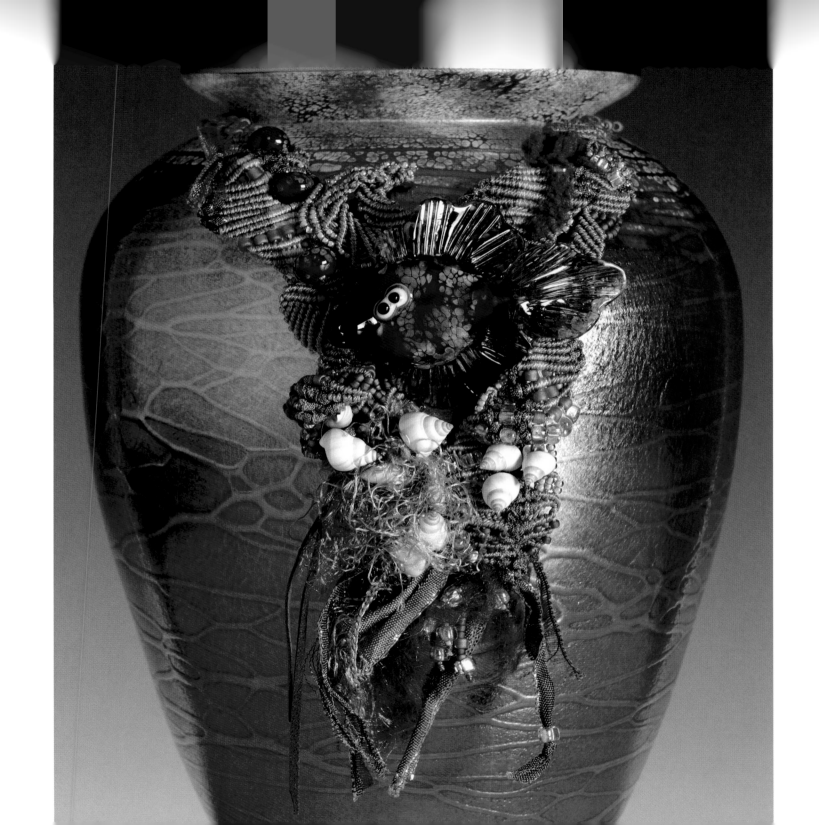

SUSAN GREEN

Translating ethnic influences into elegantly contemporary shapes, Green combines powerful focal element of carved and layered stone with delicate beading. Pearls, garnets, copper, brass, and glass. Inset shows custom clasp and signature fiber binding that gathers the many strands comfortably at the back of the neck.

Stone disc: 56mm

KELLY ANNE McKEE

Influenced by prayer strands and "costumes of different cultures particularly the styles and elements of India, Tibet and Morocco…." McKee combines tassels with carved wooden beads, faux amber, and glass in this "Prayer & Contemplation" piece.

Carved wood beads: 41mm

KATHLEEN WILLIAMS

Of her "Cleopatra" necklace Williams says: "The antique studded perfume bottle with a wicked twist I discovered years ago in an antique store. I lost my heart and paid a fortune for it and could not bring myself to part with it. I was the same with these two even more beautiful engraved silver snakes, also antique and...from Indonesia... they seem to belong together and I hope their sensuous beauty will soon adorn a beautiful bosom!" At age 94 Williams continues to "search in the garden, the woods, the street, along beaches and other places for found objects that reflect unseen and magical forces."

Snakes: 86mm

GRAZIA ZALFA

*Spirited fiber tassel complements necklace of jade
and carved serpentine. Describing her process:
"I work with the components until the design is
pleasing to my eye and I am happy."*

Tassel: 140mm

JANE OLSON-PHILLIPS

*Tendrils of linen cord surround stone butterfly resting
on serpentine slab. The designer is most drawn to the
colors of stones. She began weaving and knotting large
sculptures with beads, "…then I found linen thread
and the possibilities of making tiny knots opened up."*

Serpentine rectangle: 80mm

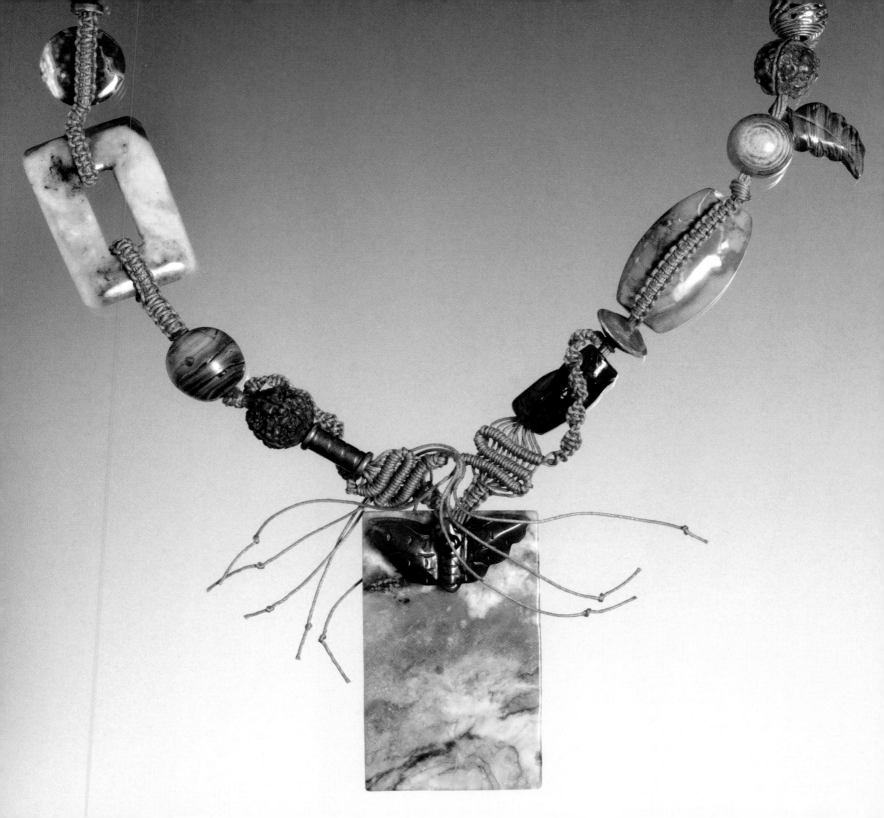

KELLY J. ANGELEY (left)

Pewter mermaid from Green Girl Studios swims through glass beads and "funky fur" yarn. Angeley's grandmother gave her a margarine tub full of beads when she was five. "Now, some thirty years later, I still sit stringing beads for hours."

Pewter pendant: 44mm

GRAZIA ZALFA

Where beads and fiber meet: donut-shaped beads wrapped with yarn. Zalfa explains: "In my life I have tried everything from batik painting to quilting, but I most enjoy sewing, wire-working, knitting and crocheting, especially with beads."

Fiber beads: 35mm

SUSAN GREEN

*Graceful twists of beads
emerge from Green's fiber
wrapping at the back
of the neck to rejoin in
another rectangle of
hand-dyed silk and rayon
cords, antique ribbons
and metallic threads.
Close-up shows subtle tones
of amber and carnelian and
the meticulous work
that characterizes
Green's designs.*

Amber beads: 5mm

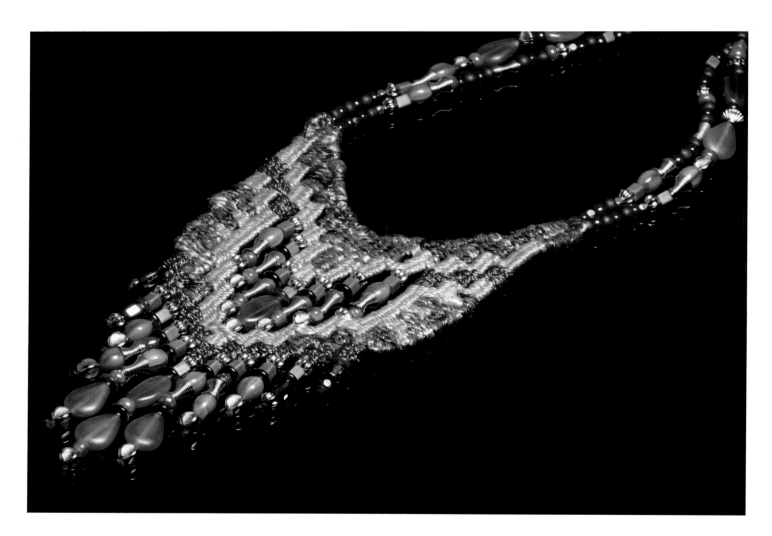

HELEN BANES

Featuring the classic needleweaving technique developed and taught by Banes, this piece titled "Scheherazade," incorporates glass and metallic beads and threads.

Bottom teardrops: 11mm

DIANE FITZGERALD

Garnet clusters and tendrils of cord accent glass leaves "to resemble a fully ripened grapevine." Fitzgerald used half-knots with nylon cord to assemble the piece.

Leaves: 29mm

METAL

Connected by wire & chain, embellished with enamel

GRAZIA ZALFA

Ethiopian copper pendant with antique Venetian trade beads. Hammered and coiled wire connects copper spacers to the beads, adding horizontal interest.

Pendant: 100mm

Copper seeping out of rocks heated by cooking fires revolutionized human society. As Oppi Untracht observes in Metal Techniques for Craftsmen, once early man "made the cause-and-effect connection, he put metal to use." Swords and plowshares replaced slingshots and digging sticks. Hammers and nails, locks and keys, sharp knives, shiny mirrors, and unbreakable beakers appeared, as did metal beads and jewelry. Among the precious metals used for beads, gold and silver and their alloys predominate. Base metals range from copper, brass, and bronze to nickel, pewter, and aluminum. Fabrication methods include forging, fusing, soldering, riveting, drawing wire, extruding tubing, and casting in molds and by the lost-wax process. Decorative techniques embrace stamping, chasing, and repoussé; engraving and etching; cutwork and appliqué; niello, plating, fire-gilding, and granulation. While initially challenging, metal can be rewarding for bead jewelry designers. What to do when you want to defy gravity? Reach for wire, sheet metal, chain, or multi-strand spacer bars. Here we show how these structural components can support your design when the draped effect is not what you're after. A metal skeleton may be exposed or concealed. Grazia Zalfa created a tumbling cascade of buttons and beads by harnessing them together with hundreds of jump rings. Don't have the bead you want? Just make it from wire! And don't forget colorful enamel and cloisonné, born of the marriage of metal and glass.

KAY WHITCOMB

Celebrating her 60th year as an enamellist, Whitcomb still recalls a lesson learned as a freshman at the Rhode Island School of Design in 1940: "Life has many challenges and persistence is the most important feature of our existence — talent is second." Her talent is abundantly illustrated here. These necklaces also attest to her persistence in completing the 21 difficult, and even hazardous, steps required to make each contemporary cloisonné bead.

Pendant: 97mm

LYNNE MERCHANT

Champagne corks dressed in copper and embellished with wire, cones, caps, and tacks. "Mad Max" reflects Merchant's mastery of metal and wire techniques as well as her interest in tribal jewelry.

Center bead: 65mm

CHRISTY KRAINESS (opposite)

Ruffled silver mesh echoes the undulating lines in crazy lace agate pendant. Yellow jade, jasper, moonstone, and freshwater pearls round out the design.

Pendant: 106mm

LYNNE MERCHANT

Coiled wire, exhibiting Merchant's virtuosity
with this medium, secures precious black Tahitian
pearls in "Wire Quagmire." Merchant wants her
"jewelry to have proper movement; to be strong,
wearable, and interesting."

Center stone: 40mm

LYNNE MERCHANT

Beach rocks caged in silver wire. Merchant learned
many techniques on a seven-year odyssey through
Africa, Yemen, Persia, Afghanistan, India, and Nepal
in the 70s. "I started by immersing myself in the local
culture...I demonstrated respect for their way of life,
and it made all the difference."

Largest rock: 40mm

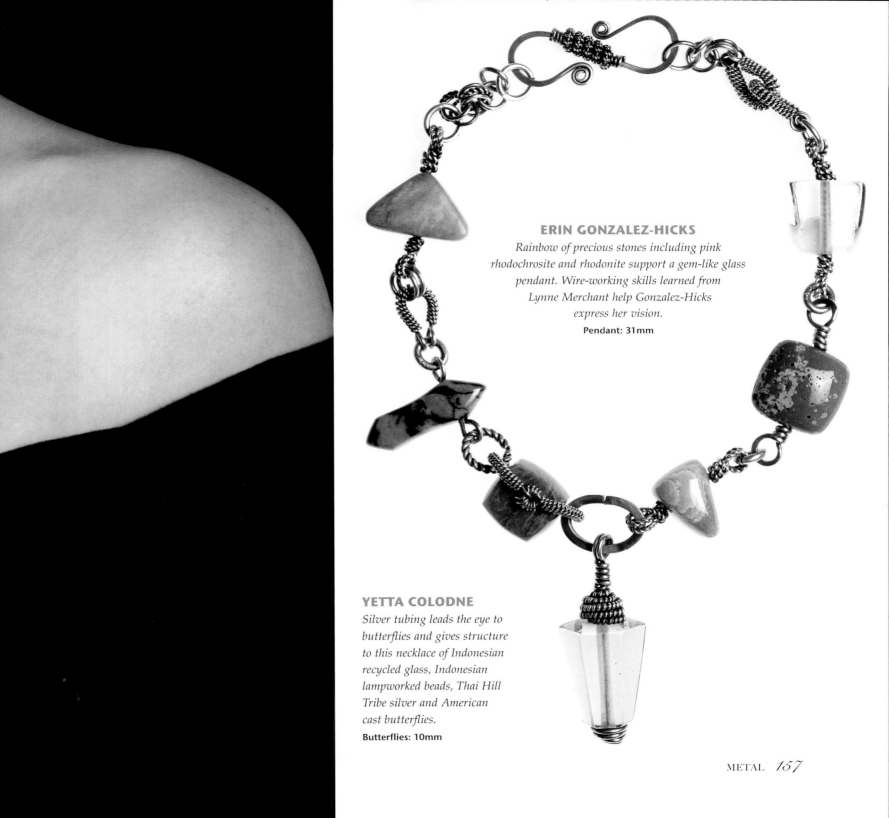

ERIN GONZALEZ-HICKS

Rainbow of precious stones including pink rhodochrosite and rhodonite support a gem-like glass pendant. Wire-working skills learned from Lynne Merchant help Gonzalez-Hicks express her vision.

Pendant: 31mm

YETTA COLODNE

Silver tubing leads the eye to butterflies and gives structure to this necklace of Indonesian recycled glass, Indonesian lampworked beads, Thai Hill Tribe silver and American cast butterflies.

Butterflies: 10mm

GRAZIA ZALFA

Network of jump rings connects mother-of-pearl buttons and drawn glass beads by David Christensen.

Striped beads: 40mm

CHRISTY KRAINESS

Aiming to be "on the cutting edge of design" Krainess also recognizes the importance of construction details for durability and functionality. Charm choker of silver wire with copper, brass, pewter, and silver dangles and beads.

Largest dangle: 12mm

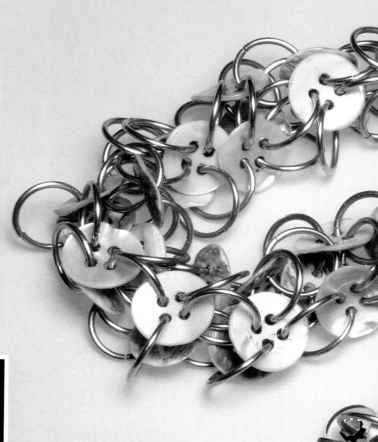

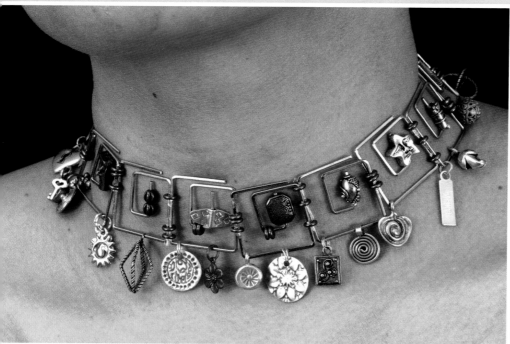

MIACHELLE DePIANO (opposite)

Exploring ways to create a distinctive style, DePiano wraps "S" shaped wire choker in pearls and gemstones. Dichroic glass pendant catches the light.

Pendant: 47mm

JENNIFER WOOD

Accomplished metalsmith and flameworker, Wood created both the silver components and the art glass beads in this necklace.

Largest glass bead: 37mm

YETTA COLODNE (opposite)

Like moons in orbit, mosaic wood beads swirl around brass tubing. "I am self-taught. Everything I do is original and executed with passion" declares Colodne.

Largest wood bead: 35mm

SIS MORRIS

After she discovered her local bead store, Morris "decided to sign up for a peyote class, got my nights mixed up and ended up attending a beaded cabochon class…I was completely hooked on beads after that." Another expression of her passion includes wirework with stone, glass, and organic materials.

Largest stone bead: 39mm

DEANNA MARIE FINOCCHIARO

Textured brass spirals used as connectors rather than drops, join brass faces outfitted with wigs of tiny freshwater pearls. Lampworked glass beads swing freely.

Spiral: 36mm

LESLIE BLOEM

Recent art school grad, Bloem submitted her metals class project blending pearls, crystals, glass, amethyst, peridot, and quartz with her enameled pendant.

Pendant: 66mm

CANDACE CLOUD McLEAN

"It's entirely my sister's fault! I was content making a living painting handmade paper… when she introduced me to BEADS!!!" Now McLean has created a line of functional bead art for the home. She enjoys the challenge of making rigid silver wire flow fluidly. Black and white glass cane beads.

Longest glass bead: 14mm

ELIZABETH HUTSELL

*Pearls, amethyst, fluorite, and Indian silver beads
punctuate 16-year-old Hutsell's mixed chain necklace.*

Bead hanging from clasp: 11mm

LILLIAN WOODBURN

*Connected to the past and looking to the future,
Woodburn has created an ancient-looking
necklace of thoroughly modern Precious
Metal Clay (PMC) and glass.*

Pendant: 74mm

GRAZIA ZALFA

*The texture and color of Zalfa's
wire-wrapped beads coordinate with
raku beads and pendant.*

Face: 110mm

CONTEMPO
Focusing on glass & other modern media

RONNIE LAMBROU
"I try to be playful and experimental," claims Lambrou. So we hope she won't mind that we used her lei-like necklace as a headdress! Lampworked beads by Jeri Warhaftig with Czech glass leaves and flowers.
Largest bead: 31mm

Infinitely adaptable and recyclable, beads never completely go out of fashion, but styles do change cyclically. After decades with the focus on mechanization, a new meeting of fire and glass in the 20th Century sparked the renaissance of glass bead-making by innovative artisans working in individual studios and small workshops. Brian Kerkvliet and fellow artisans at the Pilchuck Glass School, as well as others concentrated in Washington state's "ring of fire" and scattered throughout the U.S., pioneered the personal adornment aspect of the Art Glass movement. Their contemporary beads quickly caught the imagination of collectors. They revived ancient methods and explored new ones—drawing glass canes, grinding chevrons, using gold and silver foil, trailing and feathering, and making wound, blown, slumped, fused, and fumed glass beads. And they taught these techniques around the country, often at conferences of the Society of Glass Beadmakers. In time, some of the venerated Venetian glass houses, notorious for their secrecy, opened their doors to American artists, and some Italian glass masters visited the studios of their American counterparts, sharing knowledge to the benefit of all. Beads produced from borosilicate tubing, multicolored Moretti glass, and brilliant dichroic glass soon attracted jewelry designers, who found that these miniature masterpieces combine well with fiber as well as gemstones and metal. We close this chapter with some whimsical creations using found objects as beads. There's no limit to inspiration in search of beads!

GRAZIA ZALFA

Drawn cane beads by David Christensen. An air bubble is trapped inside a "gather" of glass, when the molten glass is pulled in opposing directions the glass elongates into a tube, with the bubble as the hole. Cutting and polishing completes the beads.

Center bead: 40mm

PENELOPE DIAMANTI

Stepped collar of rainbow-hued dichroic fused glass beads from Moontide Workshop. "I had a vision of an ancient Egyptian style collar in otherworldly materials. Creating it involved overcoming several engineering challenges: to coax the flat, rectangular beads into a curve, and to create the V in front. It was worth the effort, not just for this piece, but because I then used the techniques to create a line of similar but simpler chokers."

Dichro beads: 28mm

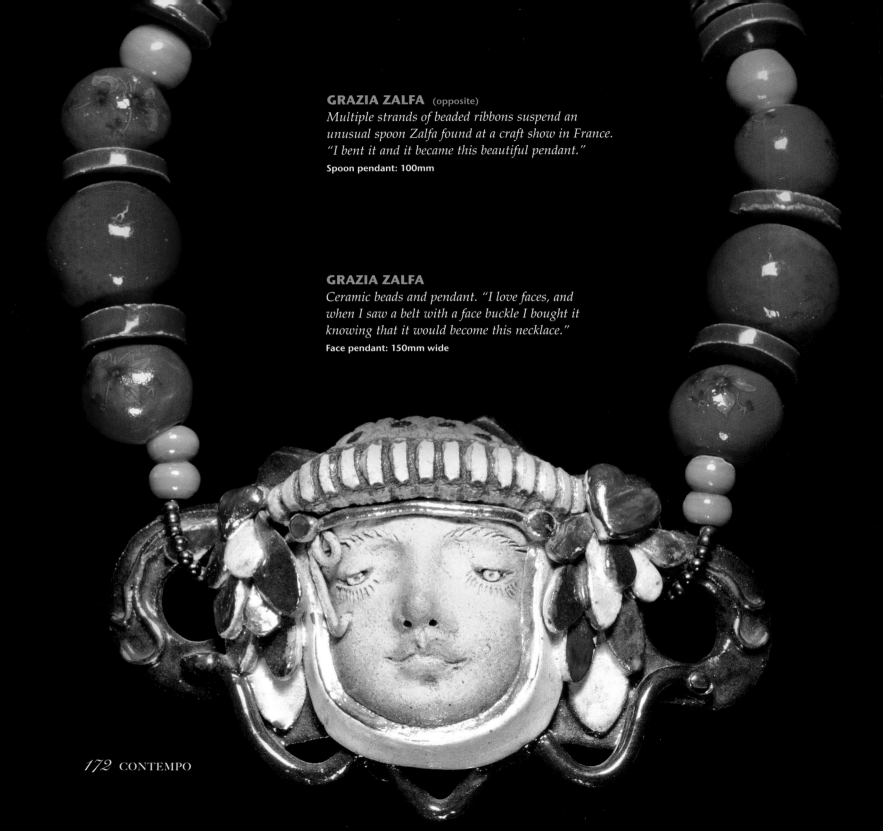

GRAZIA ZALFA (opposite)
*Multiple strands of beaded ribbons suspend an
unusual spoon Zalfa found at a craft show in France.
"I bent it and it became this beautiful pendant."*
Spoon pendant: 100mm

GRAZIA ZALFA
*Ceramic beads and pendant. "I love faces, and
when I saw a belt with a face buckle I bought it
knowing that it would become this necklace."*
Face pendant: 150mm wide

RONNIE LAMBROU

Magical lampworked fruit by Gail Crossman-Moore grows on leafy and flower-filled vines of Czech pressed glass and seed beads.

Focal bead: 58mm

INARA KNIGHT (opposite)

"Out of a large grouping of glass beads strewn about my workspace I chose pieces intuitively… building up in layers… much the same way you might create a real flower arrangement… it reminds me of the wild and random growth that takes over my garden at the end of the season." All glass beads by Knight.

Largest bead on left: 30mm

ALEX RÖEDER

Joyful combination of acrylic flowers, mother-of-pearl and metal beads, with freshwater pearls and seed beads.
"Inspiration for my designs comes from my heart and soul and evolves as I begin to work…the thrill, the anticipation, and the urge to see the finished product keeps me spellbound…until the final piece emerges."

Large open flowers: 34mm

ALEX RÖEDER

Victorian vision in lavender, this necklace was a strong candidate for the cover of this book. Röeder, who began teaching only six months after learning to bead, has won several design awards. Metal beads and leaves harmonize with Lucite flowers and freshwater pearls.

Large striped bead: 32mm

DIANNE ZACK

Thai silver with hollow glass "neolav" beads by gallery owner and beadmaker, Zack. Her "creative energy was spent focusing on the gallery's needs. My introduction to the bead world has helped me get back into the pleasure and satisfaction of making glass objects by hand. In addition, I've found a community of enthusiastic and nurturing individuals who are eager to share their addiction. I'm honored and delighted to belong to the fold."

Largest glass bead: 24mm

GRAZIA ZALFA

*Fit for a queen, two dozen strands
of vintage glass, crystals and faux pearls,
shimmer and glow as they move.*

Largest white bead: 25mm

GRAZIA ZALFA

Fused dichroic glass pendant with six fumed glass beads by Zephyr Glass. Dichroic glass was developed for the space program and enthusiastically adopted by glass beadmakers.

Pendant: 120mm long

KATHLEEN PORTER

To create this fused pendant, Porter layered clear and dichroic glass. Grinding after firing reveals the curved shape. Strung with pearls and Bali silver.

Pendant: 106mm

CHRISTINE S. GAGNON

"Blue Lagoon:" ripples of aquamarine leaves fan out from dichroic fused-glass cabochon framed with seed beads and embellished with Czech glass.

Dichroic cab: 36mm

GRAZIA ZALFA

"I was born in Trieste, Italy. In 1949 Ottavio Missoni (famed Italian textile designer) was living in my neighborhood. I am a collector of all things Missoni. In 1990 I bought a lot of his buttons that I included in this necklace, which I very much enjoyed making." Glass beads by David Christensen.

Buttons: 20mm

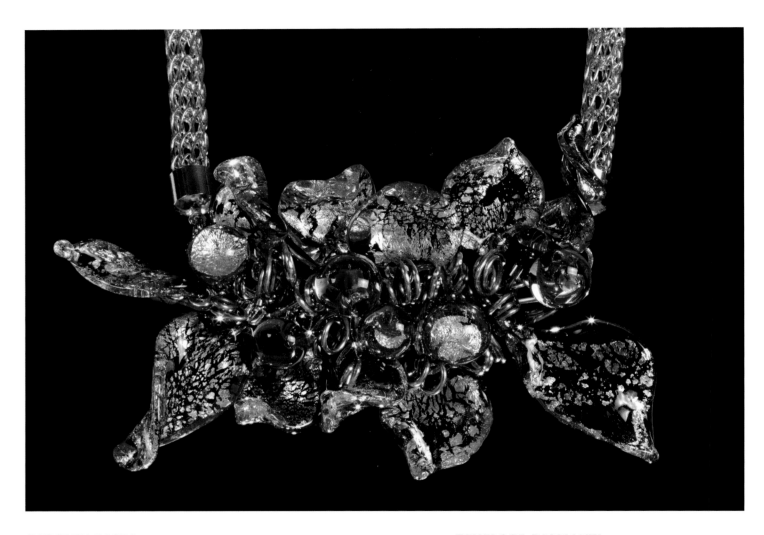

CAROLYN BAUM

Wound glass beads are usually formed around a mandrel (rod) held in the flame. Baum explains that her beads "have moved off mandrel…I now attach sterling and gold-filled wire to the bead in the flame to create small clusters of wire and glass…this allows pieces to have a very organic flavor."

Beads with silver leaf: 30mm

PENELOPE DIAMANTI

Three necklaces of dichroic glass and Czech rondelles. Pyramid centerpieces of two upper necklaces by Bruce St. John Maher. All flat beads by Moontide Workshop. Tubular and round dichroic beads from Paula Radke.

Bottom center pendant: 50mm

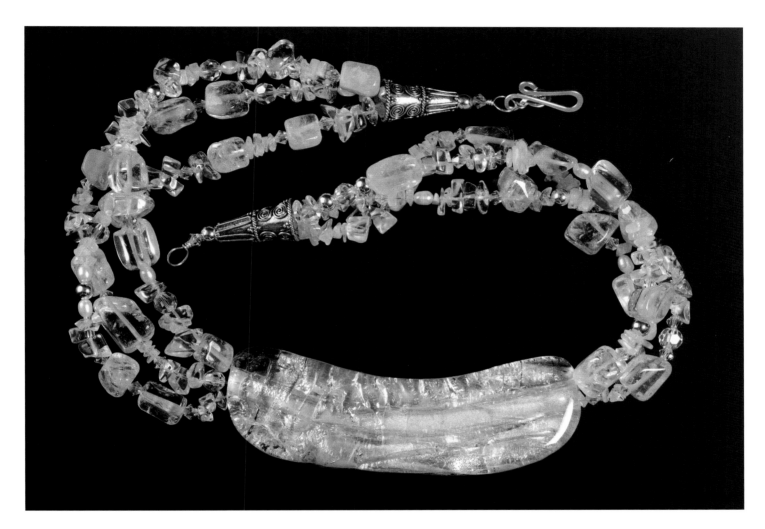

DEANNA MARIE FINOCCHIARO

Contemporary wearable perfume bottle by Ginger Saunders.
Rich assemblage of abalone shell, pearls, lamp-worked
glass, and cloisonné, elegantly joined with pewter
connectors and chain.

Vessel: 91mm

KATHLEEN PORTER

Multiple layers of clear dichroic glass were sandwiched and
fused to create the pendant. "Dichroic coatings are produced
by vacuum-depositing very thin layers of metal oxides onto
the glass, creating an optical filter that transmits specific
wavelengths of light…each dichroic glass piece has 15-45
layers of coating on it." Swarovski crystals and quartz
complete the glittering ensemble.

Dichroic bead: 92mm

PENELOPE DIAMANTI

Lapis and turquoise, prized since antiquity, meet 20th century polymer clay beads and rare purple sugilite.

Center bead: 28mm

PENELOPE DIAMANTI

Cascade of contemporary drawn glass cane beads and crystals, with vintage and new Czech glass, flows from a collar formed by two large horn-shaped drawn glass beads from Olive Glass.

Center bead on collar: 22mm

ANDREA KIERNAN

Inspired by her work on an organic lavender farm, Kiernan creates lavender necklaces from borosilicate glass. "The hollow focal bead functions as a vial, meant to be filled with the lavender plant's calming essential oil. Its wearer experiences a constant aromatherapy treatment— the next best thing to a summer walk in the fields."

Bead with stopper: 37mm

PEGGY WRIGHT

Yellow turquoise, ocean jasper, amethyst, crystals, seed beads, and lampworked beads by Dawn Tomlinson sing together in perfect harmony. Wright explains: "my work is always an exploration of color. Playing with color…has kept me hooked on beadwork for more than 15 years."

Square jaspers: 14mm

DIANE FITZGERALD

Wire holds large vintage flower beads in place against a garland of glass leaves, smaller flowers, and buds. Close-ups show detail of front and back of necklace, featuring Fitzgerald's expert work.

Big pink flowers: 23mm

DIANNE ZACK

Faceted chrysocolla with the artist's own cube beads of black, brown, and turquoise glass "cased" in clear glass for added luster. Clean lines of Thai Hill Tribe silver combine well with contemporary beads.

Center bead: 22mm

RONNIE LAMBROU (opposite)

Handmade glass leaves with Czech pressed glass flowers and leaves. Lambrou says she's "often inspired by the designs of lampwork artists. Rather than just display an important bead in a necklace, I try to expand the concept and add my own opinion and artistry to make an integrated design."

Leaves: 38mm

ANA LIVINGSTON

Let the fun begin! The last few pages of our book focus on playful combinations of beads and found objects. Cinnabar balls and lightbulb-shaped Czech pressed glass beads seem to bounce around the model's neck.

Red cinnabar: 16mm

GRAZIA ZALFA (opposite)

Zalfa stirs up red-hot chili peppers from Texas with jade leaves and beads, antique black-and-white Venetian glass trade beads, and small striped "watermelon" chevron beads from the African trade.

Peppers: 55mm

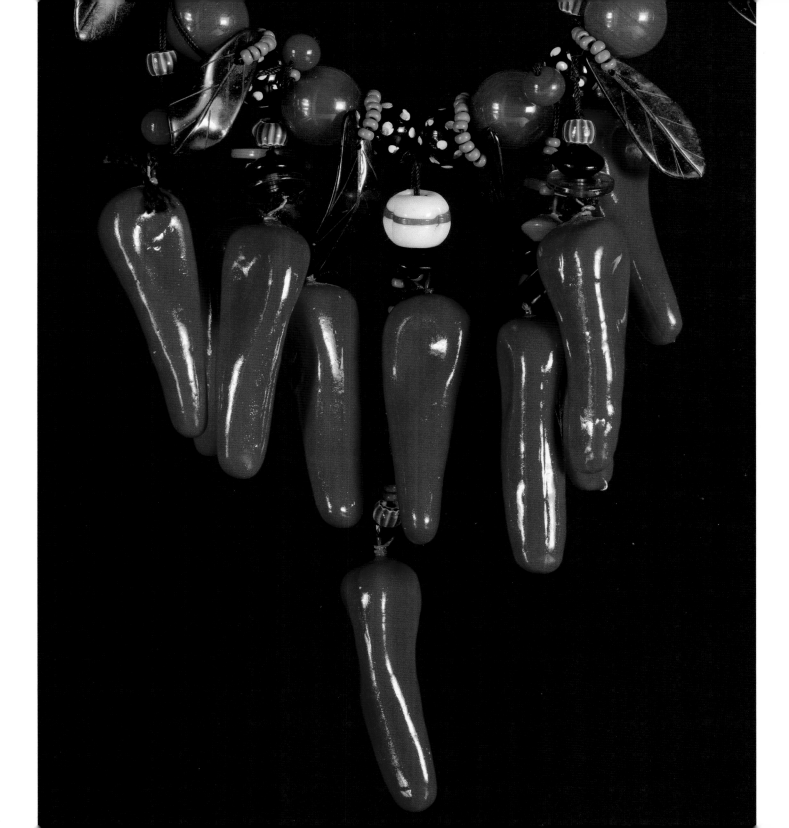

GRAZIA ZALFA

*Muted colors and soft finish of
tumbled bottle glass complement
glass and silver pendant.*

Pendant: 100mm

PHAEDRA A. TORRES

*"Open" features "found keys", buttons, serpentine, jasper, and glass.
"I've recently begun to explore using found objects in my jewelry, inspired
by my mom's large trinket collection, and my inability to
throw anything away," explains Torres.*

Center key: 57mm

GRAZIA ZALFA

A resurgence in the popularity of playing mahjong may also inspire interest in jewelry featuring vintage bakelite game pieces. With resin and faux amber.

Mahjong tile: 30mm

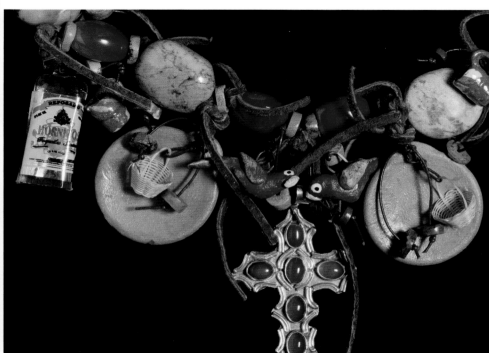

PHAEDRA A. TORRES

Mexican silver cross and miniature plates, baskets, birds, and tequila bottles conjure "Mexican Dreams" for artist Torres: "I see a piece of jewelry in everything…a pebble, a bottle cap, a buckle, a bead…I like a lot of color, large chunky beads, dangling things, fluffy things. I usually start with a basic strung necklace, and add to it until it feels complete."

Green birds: 34mm

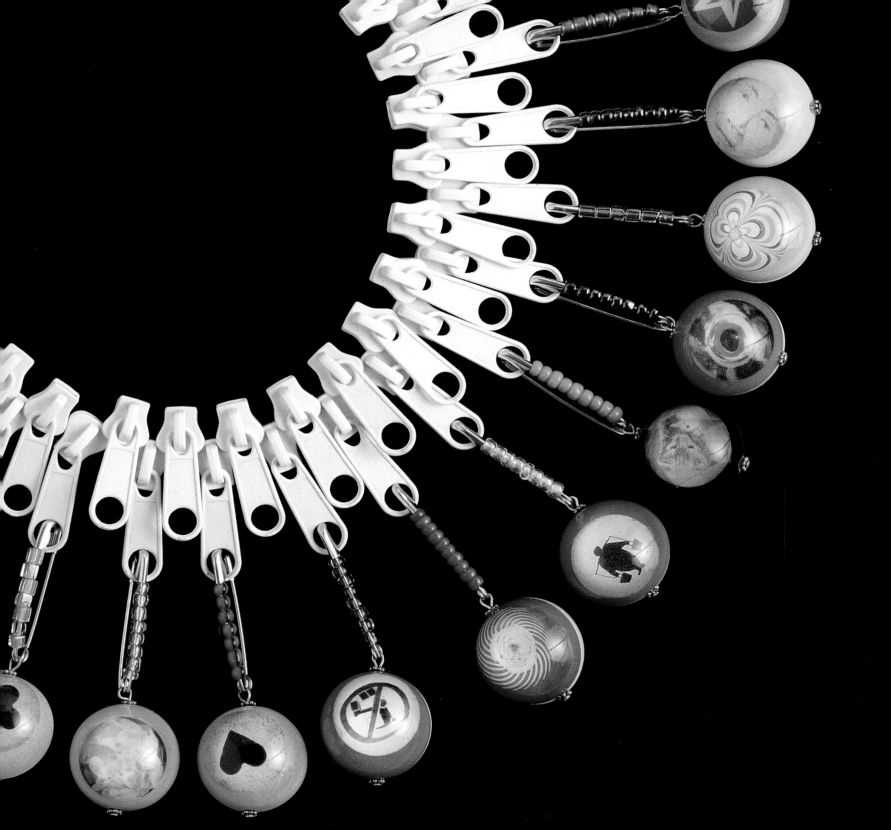

GRAZIA ZALFA

Safety pins to attach one-of-a-kind French plastic beads to zipper pulls. Zalfa found the beads in Soho, London. "There is even a Queen Elizabeth image on one of them."

Round beads: 30mm

GRAZIA ZALFA

We end on a happy note, knowing that if bottle caps and zipper pulls can make a necklace, inspiration and jewelry-making materials are truly unlimited! So be well, do good work, and have fun!

Bottle cap: 25mm

Resources

In the Washington/Baltimore area please visit our stores for beads, jewelry, and inspiration:
Beadazzled®
1507 Connecticut Ave. NW, Washington, DC 20036
501 North Charles St., Baltimore, MD 21201
Tysons Corner Center 1, McLean, VA 22102
www.Beadazzled.net

Consult the Internet for bead stores nearest you as well as for online vendors. Search the Web for up-to-date contact information for more than 50 Bead Societies and related groups.

The Bead Museums in Washington, DC (www.BeadMuseumDC.org) and Glendale, AZ (www.TheBeadMuseum.com) offer libraries and exhibits in addition to their permanent collections.

The following magazines print how-to articles, calendars of events, stories on beads and bead artists, and vendors' advertisements.

Bead and Button and *Bead Style*, Kalmbach Publishing, Waukesha, WI (www.Kalmbach.com)
Beadwork, Interweave Press, Loveland, CO (www.InterweavePress.com)
Lapidary Journal and *Step by Step*, Primedia Inc., New York, NY (www.Primedia.com)
Ornament, Ornament Inc., San Marcos, CA (OrnamentMagazine.com)

Bibliography

Apostolos-Cappadona, Diane, and Lucinda Ebersole. *Women, Creativity, and the Arts*. New York: Continuum, 1995.
Arem, Joel E. *Gems and Jewelry*. Tucson, AZ: Geoscience Press, Inc., 1975.
Audette, Anna Held. *The Blank Canvas, Inviting the Muse*. Boston/London: Shambhala, 1993.
Banes, Helen. *Fiber and Bead Jewelry*. New York: Sterling Publishing Co., Inc., 2000.
Brewster, Ghiselin, ed. *The Creative Process*. Berkeley: University of California Press, 1952.
Borel, France and John Bigelow Tayler. *The Splendor of Ethnic Jewelry*. New York: Harry N. Abrams, 1994.
Butor, Michel. *Ethnic Jewelry: Africa, Asia, and the Pacific*. New York: Vendome Press, 1994.
Cameron, Julia. *The Artist's Way*. New York: G.P. Putnam's Sons, 1992.
———. *The Vein of Gold*. New York: G.P. Putnam's Sons, 1996.
Chocron, Daya Sarai. *Healing with Crystals and Gemstones*. Boston: Weiser Books, 1986.
Conway, D.J. *Crystal Enchantments: A Complete Guide to Stones*. Berkeley/Toronto: The Crossing Press, 1999.
Daniels, Ger. *Folk Jewelry of the World*. New York: Rizzoli, 1989.
Deeb, Margie. *The Beader's Guide to Color*. New York: Watson-Guptill Publications, 2004.
Diamanti, Joyce. *Silver Speaks: Traditional Jewelry of the Middle East*. Washington, DC: Bead Society of Greater

Washington, 2002.

Dubin, Lois Sherr. *The History of Beads*. New York: Harry N. Abrams, 1987.

Duda, Margaret. *Four Centuries of Silver*. Singapore: Times Editions, 2002.

Dunning, Duangporn and Steven. *Ancient Khmer Beadmaking Art in Modern Thailand*. Mercer Island, WA: Hands of the Hills, 1990.

Ealy, C. Diane. *The Woman's Book of Creativity*. Hillsboro, OR: Beyond Words Publishing, Inc., 1995.

Eicher, Joanne B., and Lidia D Sciama. *Beads and Bead Makers*. Oxford/New York: Berg, 1998.

Fisher, Angela. *Africa Adorned*. New York: Harry N. Abrams, Inc., 1984.

Francis, Peter, Jr. *Beads of the World*. Atglen, PA: Schiffer Publishing Ltd., 1994.

———. *The Czech Beads Story*. The World of Beads Monograph Series, Vol. 2. Lake Placid, NY: Lapis Route Books, 1979.

———. *The Glass Beads of India*. The World of Beads Monograph Series, Vol. 7. Lake Placid, NY: Lapis Route Books, 1982.

———. *Indian Agate Beads*. The World of Beads Monograph Series, Vol. 6. Lake Placid, NY: Lapis Route Books, 1982.

———. *The Story of Venetian Beads*. The World of Beads Monograph Series, Vol. 1. Lake Placid, NY: Lapis Route Books, 1979.

Gabriel, Hannelore. *The Jewelry of Nepal*. New York/Tokyo: Weatherhill, 1999.

Jacobs, Julian. *The Nagas*. London: Thames and Hudson, 1990.

Johari, Harish. *The Healing Power of Gemstones*. Rochester, VT: Destiny Books, 1988.

Kalter, Johannes. *The Arts and Crafts of Turkestan*. London: Thames and Hudson, 1983.

Kock, Jan, and Torben Sode. *Glass, Glass Beads, and Glassmakers in Northern India*. Denmark: THOT Print, 1994.

Lankton, James W. *A Bead Timeline Volume I: Prehistory to 1200CE*. The Bead Society of Greater Washington, Washington, D.C., 2003.

Lewis, Elaine and Paul. *Peoples of the Golden Triangle*. London: Thames and Hudson, 1984.

Liu, Robert K. *Collectible Beads*. San Marcos, CA: Ornament, 1995.

Maisel, Eric. *The Creativity Book*. New York : Jeremy P. Tarcher, 2000.

Marascutto, Pauline B., and Mario Stainer. *Perle Veneziane*. Verona, Italy: Libreria Sansovino, 1991.

McMeekin, Gail. *The 12 Secrets of Highly Creative Women*. York Beach, ME : Conari Press, 2000.

Mella, Dorothee L. *Stone Power*. New York: Warner Books, 1988.

Menz, Deb. *Color Works*. Loveland, CO: Interweave Press, 2004.

Michalko, Michael. *Cracking Creativity: the secrets of creative genius*. Berkeley: Ten Speed Press, 2001.

Nicholson, Paul T. *Egyptian Faience and Glass*. Buckinghamshire, UK: Shire Publications Ltd., 1993.

Picard, John and Ruth. *Chevron and Nueva Cadiz Beads. Beads From the West African Trade, Vol. VII*. Carmel, CA: Picard African Imports, 1993.

———. *Millefiori Beads: Beads From the West African Trade, Vol. VI*. Carmel, CA: Picard African Imports, 1991.

———. *Russian Blues, Faceted and Fancy Beads. Beads From the West African Trade, Vol. V*. Carmel, CA: Picard African Imports, 1989.

Raphaell, Katrina. *Crystal Enlightenment. Vol. 1*. Santa Fe, CA: Aurora Press, Inc., 1985.

Stein, Diane. *Healing with Gemstones and Crystals*. Berkeley/Toronto: The Crossing Press, 1996.

Untracht, Oppi. *Traditional Jewelry of India*. New York: Harry N. Abrams, Inc., Publishers, 1997.

Ward, Fred. *Pearls*. Bethesda, MD: Gem Book Publishers, 1998.

Williams, Kathleen. *Wearable Magic*. Bethesda, MD: Kathleen Williams, 2005.

Index

JERI WARHAFTIG *Blown glass bead lined with seed beads.* **Glass bead: 30mm**

About this book

WE TOOK OFF ON A JOURNEY IN SEARCH OF INSPIRATION to find and celebrate the best beaded jewelry designers. Our goal was to document the extraordinary range of design possibilities and inspire bead artists to develop their own unique styles. Other books have documented beadwork with seed beads; so we limited this volume to necklaces using larger beads. Our call for entries was open-ended. We let the submissions we received dictate the categories. After reviewing each e-mailed entry for design criteria, color, and construction details, (yes, good photos do help) we asked artists to send selected works for further review and photography. Three months of styling and shooting later, we put the book together. This required identifying chapters to organize the work, and then achieving balance among them. We had to make some hard choices and leave out some jewelry we would have liked to include. Our next project will focus on color. We hope the success of this book will encourage established designers, as well as those who have not yet been recognized (working with seed beads and/or larger beads) to contact us through our website: www.Beadazzled.net.

About us

PHOTOGRAPHER WILLIAM L. (BILL) ALLEN served as the Editor in Chief of *National Geographic* for ten years. During his career at National Geographic as photographer, writer, and editor he covered the world for over 35 years producing hundreds of magazine articles and books on topics ranging from the discovery of the Titanic to 21st-century slavery. Under his leadership the magazine earned numerous top magazine awards. He lives in Alexandria, VA, and continues his interest in world cultures through jewelry and craft photography. More information is available from his website: www.billallenphotography.com.

AUTHOR PENELOPE DIAMANTI, jewelry designer and owner of Beadazzled® retail stores, earned an MA in Journalism and worked at National Geographic before turning full time to her bead business. Having traveled the world as the child of a diplomat, she continued her exploration as an adult, collecting and researching beads in Asia, Africa, and Latin America. She designed jewelry for galleries and museum stores before opening her three stores in the Washington/Baltimore metro area. She lives, works, and practices Tantra Yoga, in Takoma Park, MD.

ART DIRECTOR, CONSTANCE H. PHELPS brings 30 years of experience at National Geographic to this project. As Art Director/Senior Editor for *National Geographic* magazine, she was responsible for the look and feel of every page in the magazine, as well as designing over 800 stories and special newsstand issues. In addition she designed several books for their book division. She continues designing books and can be contacted at Cphelpsdesign@aol.com.

PAT DIAMANTI
Lariat of African brass with drawn glass beads by Ricky Bernstein of Penrose Glass.
Round brass: 15mm